HANS KUNG, who is presently the director of the Institute for Ecumenical Research of the University of Tübingen, Germany, has long been acclaimed a leader of the modern theological renewal. Born in Switzerland in 1928, he studied at the German College and the Gregorian University in Rome, and at the Institut Catholique and the Sorbonne in Paris.

His recent work, *The Church*, to which the present work is closely related, received widespread attention and acclaim throughout the theological world. During the winter of 1967 he was a visiting professor at Union Theological Seminary in New York and also lectured widely throughout the United States.

TRUTHFULNESS:
THE FUTURE OF THE CHURCH

Truthfulness: the Future of the Church

by HANS KÜNG

SHEED AND WARD: NEW YORK

"Part B/Realization of Truthfulness" *was translated*
from the German by Edward Quinn.

Nihil obstat:
John Coventry, S. J., Censor
Imprimatur:
✠ Patrick Casey, Vicar General
Westminster, 24 September 1968.

© *Sheed and Ward, Inc., 1968*
Library of Congress Catalog Card Number 68–9369
Manufactured in the United States of America

Contents

On the Situation

THIS BOOK is sustained by a great, unshakable hope: that the Catholic Church will emerge renewed even from the post-conciliar crises. A great deal has been achieved up to now. Greater things must still be realized in order to lead up to the future of the Church for which the Second Vatican Council has supplied goals, programs, impulses.

The situation, however, is too serious and at the same time too hopeful to allow us to conceal the crises. They exist: in the Church as a whole and in particular countries, dioceses and parishes. They are most acute in the two countries where the conciliar renewal has hitherto produced the most radical change and the finest fruits, in Holland and in the United States: precisely in this way they can be seen as inevitable crises of growth. Nevertheless they must be taken seriously. They must be taken seriously too in those countries where people largely try to conceal these crises—or at least did until the outbreak of violent clashes of opinion over Pope Paul's encyclical on birth control.

In many respects the Council was merely a catalyst. These are crises which were not created by the Council but which it merely brought into the open. Today—as is often emphasized—we are taking part not only in the end of the Tridentine age but also in the end of ecclesiastical medievalism, insofar as it was scholastic, legalistic, hierarchical, centralistic, sacramentalistic, traditionalistic,

1

exclusive and often superstitious. We must now make a great effort to compensate, in a short time, for the Catholic Church's neglect of *positive, constructive* intercourse with the trends of modern times. But at the same time (and strangely confused with all this) now, after the Council, those movements of renewal which had been partly fostered and partly hampered in the pre-conciliar age—the biblical renewal, the liturgical renewal, the lay movement and, finally, the theological and ecumenical renewal—are exerting their effects on the Church as a whole. Thus the turning point of Church history under John XXIII had been prepared in the most various ways.

In the new freedom, however, movements nourished from the most varied sources, yet still frequently limited, flowed together to make a mighty river which forced the whole Catholic Church in the Second Vatican Council into a fundamental reorientation: a positive new orientation in regard to the other Christian Churches, in regard to the Jews and the great world-religions, in regard to the secular world altogether, and thus in every respect also a new orientation of the Catholic Church in regard to what had hitherto been her own traditional structure.

But to decree such a reorientation and to realize it are two different things. Rome cannot be built, nor can it be re-built, in a day. And hence it is not at all surprising that the Catholic Church for the time being remains in the midst of a transitional stage between the pre-conciliar and the post-conciliar structures, in the passage from the past to the future. It is understandable therefore that the situation is to some degree paradoxical: everywhere, particularly at the base, strong pressure (legitimized in principle by the Council) for change and renewal of the Church's structures: hence at the same time a vigorous criticism—indeed, a rejection—of the institutional Church, so far as this represents a past which still persists. Everywhere—especially among the educated classes and the clergy—a new interest in questions of the Christian faith and a passionate demand for the pure truth of the original gospel in the new age; and thus at the same time considerable uneasiness and serious doubts about the traditional teaching of the Church on dogma and morals. Everywhere both theoretical and practical attempts at a new shaping of the liturgy and the Church's ministry in accordance with the original New Testament conception and the demands of the present time; hence simultaneously an increasing number of priests giving up their priestly office and many a crisis of vocation among theology students. Everywhere a quite new openness of the Catholic Church towards other Christian Churches and to the modern world, a new readiness to talk and to work together, and at the same time a striking incapacity on the part of the official Church to come to positive reforms.

Behind all the difficulties a crisis of leadership is involved. There are many reasons for this: not least the ambiguity of some conciliar decisions. We are now paying—as might have been foreseen—for the inconsistencies arising from the compromises (unworkable in practice) sought for the sake of the greatest possible unanimity: compromises between the conciliar majority, eager for renewal but often anxious and weak, and the curial minority, efficiently controlling the machinery of the Council. This holds not only in questions such as birth control and the recurring disdain for collegiality, but also in the test-case of the reform of the liturgy: in the Council the central question of reforming the Canon was evaded and the Latin language retained in principle as the official liturgical language of the Western Church, although exceptions were tolerated; after the Council, as a result of pressure from below, where this singular compromise could not be realized, Latin has had to be given up bit by bit in the Mass and finally entirely abandoned; at the same time, although there has been no preparation, many private attempts at reform of the Canon have to be tolerated.

The same sort of thing stands out in the fasting regulations, indulgences, cremation, freemasonry, mixed marriages, reform of the Curia, collegial participation by the "lower clergy" and the laity. Everywhere half measures and half-hearted measures, which understandably increase the uneasiness among both conservatives and progressives, strengthen the pressure on the authorities, and

will sooner or later result in further concessions—concessions
which, since they come too late, will be greeted not with gratitude
but with a grudging "At last." And will it, in the final analysis, be
any different in the case of birth control?

What is involved here is an epochal structural transformation:
to make the ecclesial community (the structure to which the conciliar catchwords such as "people of God," "charisms," "collegiality," "ministry," refer) again prevail, as against the pre-conciliar,
hypertrophic, authoritarian structure. If this conciliar transformation process is rightly understood, it becomes clear that there is a
challenge of the most positive kind to authority in the Church. But
unfortunately—and it is useful to state this quite clearly—we are
suffering in the post-conciliar Church from a notorious lack of
intellectual leadership—particularly necessary just at this time—on
the most diverse levels.

There is not really a lack of good will, although this is constantly,
but—in regard to many good pastors—unjustly suspected. But
there is a slowness, often an incapacity, to come to terms with the
difficult post-conciliar problems: for this, traditional Catholic education, theological formation, age, attachment to an obsolete system
—which, however, we ourselves represent—bureaucratic machinery
hampering officials and so many other things are responsible. At the
same time, it must gratefully be acknowledged that most ecclesiastical authorities, even before the recent experiences with student
disturbances, saw that inquisitorial, repressive, legalistic measures
cannot resolve the crisis, but at most hasten it and render it more
acute. But it is obvious that refraining from old-fashioned measures
is not enough to fill the authority vacuum.

In Rome there are many good men and there is much good will.
Various administrative reforms, simplification, tightening up, and a
more rational assignment of powers, have been set in motion; new
personalities from different nations have been called to important
posts. And yet in the whole world—really wherever you go or
from wherever you receive visits or letters—there are many who
have the impression that there is no fundamental change in Rome.
Are they wrong?

The Italian Court mentality seems to be scarcely affected. The latest creations of cardinals and curial appointments still seem to be based more on a man's previous career than upon his technical competence and intellectual formation. There are scarcely any young people in important curial posts. Nor is a plurality of nationalities the same thing as a plurality of mentalities. Theology, which was responsible for the success of the Council, is kept as far away as possible from the Roman machinery, and even now partly censored. The papal comission for reform of Canon Law, wholly dominated by canonists, works in a thoroughly unsatisfactory way (remodelling instead of complete reconstruction of Canon Law). And thus most of the Roman institutions are still in fact dominated by pre-conciliar forces which frequently indulge in an equivocal conciliar verbalism and in their concrete measures provide little evidence of being filled with the original gospel of Jesus Christ, with the conciliar spirit and with the relevant technical and worldly knowledge.

In short: for many, particularly the best-oriented and most lively, Rome—in spite of some reform-measures and new personalities— is still regarded as a center not of conciliar renewal but of pre-conciliar resistance. The failure to deal with the question of birth control, the unintelligent intervention of a hopelessly backward Roman theology against the Catechism approved by the whole Dutch episcopate, the rejection of the North American episcopate's request for permission for liturgical experiments, the negative reaction to post-conciliar theological solutions in Europe and to attempts at a thorough renewal, particularly of orders of women in the U.S.A. and the former practices of the Congregation of Missions: these and many other factors have strengthened this impression.

Some bishops' conferences, however, have been even more disappointing than Rome, precisely because more had been expected of them. Bishops who are wholly infused with the spirit of the Council have quickly become known; so too bishops' conferences like that of the Dutch, who attempted to live in accordance with their responsibility. Naturally, something has happened everywhere.

That is not to be denied. But on the other hand the saddening fact cannot be overlooked that some bishops' conferences, which in Rome boldly demanded reforms, have since largely failed at home in the reform of their own Churches. This is the result of insecurity, passivity, fear of Rome, persistence in long-obsolete ecclesiastical positions and privileges (especially in education and politics), of pre-conciliar mentality, theological ignorance, personal animosity towards pertinent criticism, and irrelevant and ineffective reaction to suggestions for reform from their own Churches.

Right up to the externals—clothes and paternalistic style—it often seems as if nothing decisive has changed; that the conciliar renewal in all essentials has been wound up. And, although individual bishops in their own dioceses in some cases proceed very openly, boldly and progressively, in the bishops' conferences they seem to be largely tamed. In view of the abundance of concrete tasks, it seems to many very sad that there are individual bishops' conferences which in the four years of the Council were leading in the progressive conciliar majority and in the three years since the close of the Council have not carried through consistently a single bold reform-measure in their own provinces.

There are other facts which are particularly depressing. On the one hand, Rome has refused to accept the resignations of bishops who are too old according to the directives of the Council (by comparison with corresponding secular positions seventy-five is an extremely high age limit), especially if it was a question of bishops true to the Roman line, while the resignation of others was only too readily accepted and up to a point provoked. On the other hand, in the post-conciliar Church, especially for sees of particular importance, bishops have been appointed (often against the express wish of clergy and laity who should have been consulted), who were frequently regarded even by their own clergy as very average personalities and unsuited to the post-conciliar age; well-meaning and pliant, but incapable of controlling the situation and giving intellectual leadership (often even of maintaining the status quo, which seems important to Rome; even in the Roman Curia no one ever thinks of restoring the status quo ante).

Quite honestly, there is no intention here of making a personal attack upon anyone, of belittling any positive achievement. There is in Rome and among the bishops endless good will, and therefore much is done well. Only it must be clearly stated: so much could and absolutely ought to have been done better. We urgently need today a *renewed* authority, aware in a new way of what is involved in the original Christian message and required at the present time. We are not speaking against authority in the Church, but for it. For the consequence of the negative side of post-conciliar developments here described, which could be corroborated by innumerable details, is unfortunately (and that is why we must speak so clearly about it) a dangerously progressive erosion of papal and episcopal authority and a considerable disturbance of confidence between the hierarchy and the most lively members of the Church, both among the clergy—and not only the younger ones—and among the laity— and not only the intellectuals.

To be sure, it is understandable that the representatives of the hitherto dominant organizational structures should be experiencing special difficulties in deducing for themselves the necessary practical consequences of the goals, programs and new attitudes on which they decided in the Council. Reaction to reforms of the system varies, of course, with one's place in the system. Yet if those who are responsible for freedom and order in the Church do not act, it will scarcely be possible even now to prevent many in the Church from bothering less and less about these authorities and themselves, taking steps to realize the conciliar programs, goals and attitudes.

In the private sphere of the individual person (for instance, marital morality) this is already happening to a large extent. It is already beginning to appear on all sides in the public life of the Church. There are warning signs of this: the more critical mood and demand for freedom in theology, the unrest of many seminaries, priests organizing themselves in something like trade unions, the rebellions of many individual priests against certain measures of their bishops in many different countries, the restlessness of Catholic student groups, the new groupings of many laymen, the crisis in the Catholic press and, finally, the negative reactions to both the papal *Credo* and the encyclical on birth control. If these developments are not to assume proportions dangerous for the Church herself, then the bishops, instead of mainly putting the brakes on as hitherto, must advance boldly and decisively as pastors in their Churches, as they did so impressively and refreshingly in Rome in the sphere of theory and in general. In this way the present tensions and conflict—which cannot be concealed, still less suppressed—will not lead to dissolution, but to a new integration.

In order to overcome the present crisis of leadership in the Church, one thing is particularly necessary. The success of Vatican II was largely due to the constructive co-operation of the bishops with the theologians, who in most cases prepared the good speeches and suggestions of the bishops and worked out the conciliar documents on which the bishops had to pronounce. The failures of Rome and various post-conciliar bishops' conferences must be ascribed largely to the lack of constructive co-operation between bishops and theologians at the level of the diocese, the nation and the whole Church. The Curia and many bishops' conferences have incapsulated themselves, as in pre-conciliar times: they like congenial advisers and solitary decisions. Although authority today can still prevail only in virtue of technical competence and co-operation in partnership, many have taken refuge in the older absolutist forms and habits. They withdraw from discussion, rely on their bureaucracy and speak from this sphere in "words of pastoral direction," without noticing that in this way they are isolating themselves more and more and simply inviting criticism.

In positive terms, the "cleavage between ecclesiastical institution and theological reflection" (E. Schillebeeckx), frequently deplored today, must be overcome in a critical-constructive co-operation of pastors and teachers in the Church resting on mutual respect. Pastors and teachers each have their own function of leadership; theologians must not want to play at being bishops, nor bishops to play at being theologians. According to Paul, the charisms in the Church are various; not everyone has several and no one has them all. It is best for the people who make up the Church when all charisms find expression in freedom and love and the Spirit is nowhere extinguished.

The whole Church then is challenged to fulfill the promises in the Council's program. And they can be fulfilled. If we have spoken here so openly about Rome and the bishops, it was not in order to indulge in negative criticism, but in the hope and firm confidence that the fraternal appeal will be heard, understood and vigorously answered.

It would, however, be a bad thing if theologians could once again be reproached for not having recognized the signs of the time or for thinking only in the privacy of their own studies of what must be cried out from the roof-tops. What so many are thinking and wishing, without being able to get a hearing, must be expressed and formulated above all by theology in the public life of the Church, critically sifted and precisely stated in the light of the message of Jesus Christ. This is not said as a result of a theological "missionary fanaticism"—as some might suspect—but from a modest sense of theological duty which, in this service to men who suffer and hope in the Church and the world, may not allow itself to be put off by those to whom the service is inconvenient, because they will have to change themselves.

It comes from an awareness of theological duty and—let this too be noted quite unsentimentally—out of love for this Church to which the whole wearisome labor of theology is devoted; a Church which, as God's pilgrim people, needs no deifying, flattering, idealistic adulation but most certainly needs a love which is strong, suffering and hopeful on the part of those who are concerned, affected, responsible: a love which need not apologize for telling the truth but lives for the unfeigned truth. Such love—as with Moses and the prophets, with Jesus and Paul—does not exclude a holy anger. This holy anger—that is, just anger based on personal awareness of evil—really needs rehabilitation in the Church today. Too many tame and lame—sometimes even opportunist—scribblers have praised the gentleness of Jesus, entirely forgetting his anger, which was never directed against the poor sinners of this world but against hypocrisy, outward show of piety

and legalistic morality, the indolence and stubbornness of the
religious establishment of the time. And if, with all due modesty,
even professors of theology are not to be denied all prophetic
gifts, for them also within the people of God in the Church it will
be a question of a double mandate, in which both positive and
negative have to be realized in virtue of love: "to pluck up and
to break down. . . . to build and to plant" (Jer. 1.10).

With the second Vatican Council came the "moment of truth"
for the Catholic Church: hence in this book all that has to be said
on the future of the Church and the Church of the future is linked
with the theme of *truthfulness*. The treatment of the subject itself
will bring out in concrete form the fact that this is one, if not *the
central,* standpoint from which the problems of the post-conciliar
Church, her great anxieties and her still greater hopes, must be
seen. If some negative judgments have to be made, then it is always
for the sake of the positive aspect, of building and planting. The
unrealized impulses, intentions and programs of the Council, which
is rightly understood not according to the letter but the spirit, ought
to be realized in a sincere, thorough and consistent fashion. Or,
better: the Church ought again to correspond more to the message
of him to whom she constantly appeals and, precisely as renewed
in this way, be prepared for mankind at the present time, and indeed in the future.

If the theologian then wishes to accomplish faithfully his pioneer-
service, he must be prepared for dangerous walking on the edge of
the precipice. The author of this book is aware of his grave
responsibility in the Church. In the present situation he does not
attach any importance to a rigid adherence to apparently safe
traditions. Abysses are not crossed by staying on the heights: there
is no need to develop this. But neither does he attach any importance to wild, unplanned, hectic onrushing. An unrestrained search
for utopias may lead us to a wall of rock, a precipice, from which
we are unable either to advance or retreat.

Hence some traditionalists, particularly in the ecclesiastical
establishment, will not be satisfied with this book: they would prefer to incapsulate the Church under the bell-jar of a pseudo-eternity,

sterilized and free from the germs of human history, so that they could continue undisturbed, comfortably muddling through in the old style. But there are also some Utopians, particularly among theological journalists who—with the best intentions—will turn anything good into an absolute, who in their justified aversion from traditionalism depreciate tradition in faith and doctrine, in justified aversion from institutionalism depreciate the institutional element in Church and constitution: they are much concerned about the secular world and little about the original Christian message, neglect serious biblical scholarship and would like to replace theology with dilettante sociology, psychology or philosophy; or they try to turn our congregations into political debating clubs.

We do not want either of these approaches: in the last resort neither is to the advantage of men, nor do they correspond to the program with which the Church of Christ first went into action. Provided that everything is *rightly* understood and realized, we must therefore agree with the warning of Pope Paul VI (April 25, 1968):

Renewal, yes; arbitrary changes, no. An ever living and new history of the Church, yes; an historicism dissolving the traditional binding force of dogma, no. Theological integration in accordance with the teachings of the Council, yes; a theology conforming to free, subjective theory and following often hostile sources, no. A Church open to ecumenical love, responsible dialogue and the recognition of Christian values among separated brethren, yes; an irenicism which dispenses with the truth of faith, no. No also to the inclination to accept certain negative principles which have fostered the severance of so many Christian brethren from the cult of unity of the Catholic community. Freedom of religion for all in the sphere of civic society, yes; yes, too, to personal freedom to belong to a religion according to the choice of one's own conscience; no, however, to freedom of conscience as a criterion for religious truth without the support of the genuineness of a serious and authorized magisterium.

What the author regards as the positive element in the Church will not be found in the present book. It is expounded in his work

The Church. Regardless of what is considered to be modern just
at the present time, in that book strict theological method is applied
to an exact analysis, in the light of the New Testament message,
with all its consequences for the concrete composition of the
Church, of what the Church is in virtue of her origins and what she
ought therefore to be also under changed conditions in our own
day. What is there developed—the program implicit in her origin,
of a Church which in a new age corresponds to the Gospel of
Jesus Christ—is given concrete form in the present book and applied in relation to some central post-conciliar problems and both
theoretical and practical tasks. If these questions are clarified, then
it is easier to draw further conclusions for the concrete ministry
of the Church to human beings in the secular world of political
realities.

For that very reason this book is written for *all* those to whom
the Church is important. For us categories and classifications are
of no account if they are meant as labels and in an exclusive sense:
conservative-progressive, right-left, old-young . . . ! There are
devout elderly women in the Church who have grasped the meaning
of the liturgical reform better than many a younger college gradu-
ate, proud of his education. Conversely, many a supposedly terribly
progressive theological avantgardist is not at all aware of how he
is merely leading the Church again into a new captivity. On the
one hand, there are progressives who are in some respects de-
plorably reactionary and conservatives who in many respects are
terribly fashionable. On the other hand, conservatives who are in
principle open-minded towards the future and progressives who live
entirely on the great, genuine tradition of the Church.

With all the differences of emphasis, of trends and groupings,
which exist also in the Catholic Church as a result of the new
conciliar freedom, we must not drift apart from one another.
Tensions must not become divisions. We can all learn from one
another. And certainly we must not lapse into the old Protestant
fault of mutual private excommunication, nor—taking the opposite
stand—repeat the mistake of pre-conciliar Catholicism, of imposing

moral disqualifications. Progressives, particularly now when they are frequently "in power," ought to consider it an honor to defend "conservatives" whenever these are calumniated or when they are ridiculed just because of their conservatism. Thus it must be possible not only to preserve unity but to realize it anew in mutual tolerance, in listening and understanding, in mutual aid and in working together. That at any rate is how this book should be understood: as the contribution of a theologian who does not feel tied to any party, but who would like to serve the Church, to serve human beings, and who—for that very reason—speaks the truth openly, even when it is not flattering, conscious that only someone who practises truthfulness in his writing is justified in writing about truthfulness in the Church.

The book arose out of a total vision which has become clearer in the course of time. The first, basic part began as material for a lecture before bishops and theologians in Rome towards the end of the Council; then it was used in an English version for a lecture on the occasion of the centenary celebrations of the Pacific School of Religion in Berkeley (California) and for both the West Memorial lectures of Stanford University (California) and numerous other American and European universities. This part was left unchanged for that and other reasons, which are explained at the beginning of the second part. The second part is made up of the lectures which I first gave in Tübingen for an audience drawn from all faculties and then in Spring 1968, as Harry Emerson Fosdick Visiting Professor at Union Theological Seminary in Riverside Church in New York. The fact that so many felt the lectures to be of real help has encouraged me to publish them.

Nor can I be grateful enough to the many people, in and outside the Catholic Church, who in myriad ways have offered their positive reaction and encouragement as well as their constructive criticism. They have thereby helped me to carry the often heavy burden of the theologian in a spirit of joy.

The publication, in the meantime, of Pope Paul's *Credo* as well as his encyclical on birth control has unexpectedly sharpened the

timeliness of this book, especially Part B, Chapters 7 and 8. Apart
from references to the encyclical, I have made no changes. Only in
the Appendix is the public position I have taken in connection with
the encyclical literally reprinted under the title which I should also
have liked to have written over the chapters I have just mentioned:
"A Helping Word."

HANS KÜNG

Tübingen, August, 1968

I/The Passion for Truthfulness in the Twentieth Century

ONE DAY during a session of the Second Vatican Council, one bishop passed another a note, which then made the rounds. The message read: "Senatus non errat, et si errat, non corrigit ne videatur errasse." (The Senate does not make mistakes, and if it does, it does not correct them, lest it should seem to have erred.)

Question: Whom did the bishop mean by the sentence, which brought a sly and knowing smile to the lips of the other bishops? Did he mean the senate of the ancient Romans or the Senate of the United States or the senate of a university or . . . ? But let us begin with the beginning.

The twentieth century is full of all kinds of insincerity, dishonesty, lies, hypocrisy. Isn't it possible for our century—with the help of vast technical means—to lie better than any previous ones? The giant propaganda machines of the totalitarian systems bear witness to this; the vision of George Orwell, in his futuristic novel, *1984*, of a Ministry of Truth with the task of counterfeiting history is basically no more than an extrapolation of past experience. But even in our democracies we have brought "the manipulation of truth" in politics, news media, and propaganda to a high degree of perfection.

And yet when we sum up the characteristics of this twentieth century we certainly cannot ignore one feature: a new passion for

15

truthfulness. The twentieth century displays a feeling for straight-forwardness, honesty, originality, genuineness, sincerity, and truth-fulness in the ultimate sense of the word which the nineteenth century (a period ending roughly with the First World War) did not have. This idea is so familiar to us all that we need only call to mind a few key points: Just think of modern *architecture* and the style of "New Realism" which in this century brought the artificial-ity of Historismus, neo-Classic, neo-Gothic and neo-Romantic to an end; this modern architecture, as represented by Gropius, Behrens, Mies van den Rohe, Wright, Le Corbusier and Saarinen, demands construction without artifice and the honest use of ma-terials—concrete should be treated as concrete, wood as wood, and glass as glass—an architectural style formed by purpose, purely functional, which even at its most audacious remains sober, objec-tive and unsentimental.

Think of modern *sculpture,* which, since Maillol, has gone back to the basic elements—cone and sphere, rhombus and block—con-cerned with ultimate simplicity and abstractions, and in cubism striving with an almost exaggerated strictness and sobriety to achieve pure form. Rather than use the painted plaster of the nineteenth century, contemporary sculptors have turned to raw iron, wire or various mechanical elements.

Think of modern *painting* and the thirst of someone like Henri Matisse and the other Fauvists for vivid, unadulterated color—*couleurs pures*—clear graduations and bold contrasts. Closely linked with this is a rejection—even in illustrations and posters—of the spatial illusion through which the plane surface is not treated as a plane. Everywhere, even in surrealism, new areas of reality, of human existence, are being illuminated, though in forms which are, to be sure, often bizarre.

Think of the *novels* and *poetry* of the twentieth century, so often marked by biting honesty, probing the weaknesses of the individual soul and society; and the striving in motion pictures for honest style, from the Italian neo-realism to the *cinema-vérité* and the *nouvelle vague.*

Think of modern *psychology* seeking to understand man in his actual reality, delving into his unconscious through the analysis of his dreams in order to discover the dark sides of his being, to assist him in achieving truthfulness in regard to himself and his environment, to prevent—as C. G. Jung says—the "persona" from masking the true self.

Think of contemporary *sociology* destroying social taboos, attempting to analyze by means of its manifold methods—not the least of which is the public opinion poll—the actual situation of human society, not shrinking from the most difficult questions, whether of religion or human sexuality.

Finally, let us think of philosophy: Marxism, for example, seeking the practical means of freeing man from his alienation in society; the philosophy of Heidegger or Sartre, seeking to deliver man from depravity, dishonesty, superficiality, insincerity—from *mauvaise foi* to authenticity and sincerity. The idea of the genuine, which is related to sincerity, so much valued by Nietzsche, is rendered by Sartre and Gide as *authenticité*, and they translate Heidegger's term *Eigentlichkeit* by the same word.

Not only the literature, arts, and sciences of the twentieth century, however, but also the attitude of man in daily life is marked by a new passion for a sincerity which has risen above the hypocrisy of the Victorian and *wilhelmenischen* eras. Whether we like it or not, people today are willing to forgive almost any sin as long as it is committed with honest conviction. They are instinctively suspicious of high-flown rhetoric, of anything suggesting phoniness or a façade, of affectation in speech, dress or style of life. They accept no merely formal authority whose claims are not backed up by solid evidence; they accept only that authority which demonstrates its integrity by an actual competence. Hence they have a spontaneous liking for men who are genuine, who are completely themselves: people like John F. Kennedy, who was different from so many politicians in this respect, or John XXIII, who was different from so many churchmen, who was completely authentic, completely himself, completely sincere.

It is not an exaggeration to say that the twentieth century is marked by a passion for truthfulness. Of course there are, as we have already said, lies and hypocrisy in our century, and the drive for sincerity can be corruped by sensationalism and exhibitionism in literature, the press, motion pictures and even in scholarship. But the feeling contemporary man has for sincerity is nonetheless something great, something to be wondered at, something which sets men free. It moves many wise old men to say that young people today are better, not because they make fewer mistakes but because they are more sincere.

And the Church? If the foregoing remarks are true of the world today, what can we say of the Church?

I can answer directly for the Church of which I am a member, the Catholic Church, but everyone can apply the analogy for himself to the other Christian Churches—in one way or another, truthfulness is a problem which concerns every Church. We may say, with satisfaction, that the drive for sincerity has not stopped at the doors of the Churches. In the Churches as well we see more sincerity. To consider a few points: Though this varies from country to country, the painted plaster and worthless art is more and more being cleared out of the churches. One finds increasingly modern, simple, more authentic, functional architecture, sculpture and painting. For the last few decades there has been a church art which can serve as a model for the profane arts.

Unusually frank, realistic theater, literature and films are no longer so readily condemned by the Church. Once again there are serious writers who are consciously Christian.

Even in the Church—to a greater or lesser extent—the findings of psychology, sociology and philosophy are being taken seriously; in fact they are frequently being used in the Church. Among both lay people and clergy there is a new feeling for constructive self-criticism, sincerity and truthfulness in all areas of Church life.

There has also come into being in the Church an instinctive rejection of everything which prevents the full expression of the truth: inquisitions, denunciation, censorship—every kind of coercion of opinion or belief.

This sincerity, this truthfulness, has not stopped short at the doors of the Church because its members live in the world also and are increasingly less ready to accept a schizoid existence between the Church and the world. Nevertheless there is no doubt that the Second Vatican Council has been of greater significance in this respect than we may have realized. It has brought the Catholic Church into a relationship of greater truthfulness with the other Christian Churches, the Jews, the other world-religions and the modern world in general—and, last but by no means least, with itself. The Catholic Church has cause for rejoicing in this new truthfulness, but rather than resting content with what it has achieved it must now strive courageously and energetically to bring this development to completion, and this for special reasons. If we want to avoid falling into an oversimplified apologetic, we must not overlook the fact that very few of the decisive movements toward truthfulness—whether beginning in the nineteenth or the twentieth century—have come from the Church itself. This is not self-explanatory. It was not always the case and could very well have been otherwise. If we consider again the same key points:

The great innovators in modern architecture, painting and sculpture, in contrast to earlier times, have not come from the milieu of the Church; we have followed in the wake of the secular world's innovations and later appropriated them for ourselves. The situation in *literature* is somewhat better, but the consciously Christian authors, especially the Catholics, are proportionately less important than the others. Many, such as Graham Greene and Evelyn Waugh, were converts, and the best among them were often the least appreciated by the Church of their time. Léon Bloy, Karl Muth, Georges Bernanos, Charles Péguy and Reinhold Schneider stood in opposition to the Church which they loved.

The founders of modern *psychology*, especially of psychoanalysis, had no link with the Church; Freud and Adler were Jews, and C. G. Jung, a Protestant, felt no special bond with his Church. Even the first signs of the *social justice* which shaped our century originated not primarily in the Church but among the Church's opponents, the socialists and communists. True, one can count in the Church a number of precursors of her present social teaching, but we should not forget the main figures: two significant dates—

1848 the Communist Manifesto, but not until 1891 the first social encyclical, *Rerum Novarum*. Here, too, we were followers. The same is true for other scholarly disciplines, including *philosophy*: the really important intellects were not of the Church. Heidegger and Scheler, originally members of Catholic religious orders, left the cloister and had nothing to do with the Church thereafter. Compared to Heidegger and Scheler, Jaspers and Sartre, the Jewish philosophers Husserl and Bergson, and many in the English-speaking world as well, names like Marcel, Blondel and Maritain provide no sufficient basis for a convincing apologetics.

There are whole areas of scholarship into which committed Christians—and especially Catholics—have dared to venture only by way of exception, seldom achieving excellence; one thinks, for example, of comparative religion, sexual research, psychoanalysis . . . ! For a long time all these areas were considered "dangerous" and to be avoided. The age-old suspicion of the Catholic Church towards the natural sciences has radically limited the number of Catholics in this field. And generally, in pluralistic societies, the number of Catholic professors and students is shockingly low.[1] Even in Catholic countries, the universities are often anticlerical and opposed to the Church. All this is not without cause, and it is connected with the question of truth and sincerity.

What should our answer be? Not defeatism or pessimism—we have already noted the positive elements in the Church's development, and this could be extended further. And certainly not conquest of the kind sought by an aggressive Catholicism of the past, which would apply every worldly means—propaganda, church pressure groups, the use of money—to control literature, motion pictures and research. Our initial response to this unhappy situation should be calm reflection, especially about its causes, among which the lack of truthfulness in the Church—in all the Churches, but especially in the Catholic Church—is foremost. By truthfulness we mean much more than mere sincerity or honesty in the narrow sense.[2] We mean, first of all, that basic attitude through which individuals or communities, in spite of difficulties, remain true to themselves without dissimulation and without losing their integrity: a genuine candor with oneself, with one's fellows and with God, a genuine candor in thought, word and deed. By "Church," however, we mean the entire community of believers, the whole people of God. We also mean in particular those who serve the Church in a special ministry and thus have a special responsibility for the truthfulness of the Church. We mean not only the Catholic Church but every Church which sees these questions as relevant for itself.

NOTES

1. The "Catholic education deficit" is an internationally established phenomenon (cf., for example, for Germany the investigations of K. Erlinghagen, *Katholisches Bildungsdefizit in Deutschland,* Freiburg im Breisgau, 1965; for U.S.A. R. H. Knapp and H. P. Godrach, *Origins of American Scientists,* Chicago, 1952). Three facts are typical of this situation: (1) among educated classes the percentage of Catholics is smaller than that of Protestants. (2) Catholics are particularly unrepresented among those who take up a scholarly career. (3) A strikingly large number of Catholics avoid the study of the natural sciences and technology in favor of arts. Together with social and political factors, the reason for this is said to be above all ideological inhibitions, the uncertain attitude of the Catholic Church to modern science and the secular world (authoritarian-ecclesiastical and theological traditionalism).
2. Cf. below under B II.

II/Historical Background to the Disregard for Truthfulness

IF THERE has been a lack of truthfulness in the Churches, it cannot properly be attributed to the failure of the individual through fear or cowardice, although this has, of course, played its part. It is due much more to a long process in the history of theology and of the Church which has developed certain basic attitudes, which in turn have formed the individual. It is necessary for us to see the historical background. I should like to call attention to three moments.

a. The first moment: the sweeping disregard of truthfulness in moral theology. It is a matter of some importance whether or not there is a natural place in a theological system for a particular object of interest and whether that place is central or merely peripheral; in the ordinary treatment of the virtues, truthfulness appears only around the periphery. Truthfulness is not one of the "theological" virtues (faith, hope and love). That is not unreasonable, although faith in the *Deus qui verax est,* the God who is truthful, could be decisively more significant than the external guarantee of the rational-intellectual proofs of faith offered by our fundamental theology. Truthfulness, which for the modern man is a basic virtue, does not even belong to the "cardinal virtues" (not to be confused with the "virtues of the cardinals"!). In the classical scheme, the four cardinal virtues are justice, fortitude, temperance and that virtue which in the Church often appears to be the queen, the heart or "cardo," of the cardinal virtues: prudence. Truthfulness has no place of its own in this system but must be subsumed under some other virtue.

Over and above this: In the history of moral theology, truthfulness is considered from a negative point of view. Even Augustine wrote no treatise *De veracitate* ("On veracity"), but rather *De Mendatio*, "On the nature of falsehood." As he, the great theologian and pastor, remarks in the very first chapter, falsehood is for him "the big question which confronts us in daily affairs." [2] From then on, truthfulness was approached negatively; seen, for the most part, one-sidedly, from the standpoint of falsehood. As if hypocrisy, distorted attitudes and falsified reality were not at least as dangerous and widespread a denial of truth as falsehood! One can be fundamentally untruthful without ever having told a lie; while the lie has to do with individual statements, untruthfulness has to do with the very heart of the person. Furthermore, Augustine, one of the most truthful theologians in the history of the Church, did not take a purely theoretical approach to the problem of truth and falsehood; rather, his was a very existential position: falsehood was concerned with the falsification of the truth for personal gain. [3]

Thomas Aquinas's way of looking at the matter is much more objective and intellectual. We shall not discuss it in detail, but limit ourselves to the following observation: for Thomas, the intention to deceive (*cupiditas, intentio fallendi*), is necessary to the act of lying, to the *perfectio* of the falsehood. The nature of falsehood lies in the *falsitas formalis*, in the willing to say something objectively false (*voluntas falsum dicendi*). [4] Thus Thomas subsumed veracity under justice, inasmuch as, through the lie, that which is owed (*debitum*) is not rendered. Therewith was laid the foundation of that casuistry in regard to truthfulness which became especially evident during the Counter-Reformation: a morality employing a whole catalogue of distinctions (*restrictio mentalis—* mental reservations in the narrowest and broadest sense). Although recognizing the fundamental sinfulness of lying, this morality allowed almost every possible equivocation and dissimulation, provided one found the right distinction. Inevitably this unlimited casuistry did violence to the standard of truthfulness itself, since one was less concerned with truthfulness than with the question: How can I achieve my goal without telling a formal lie?

In this way, for reasons too many and various to be gone into here, the sixth commandment was inordinately overrated, while the eighth commandment was peculiarly underrated. According to the manuals of moral theology in the post-Tridentine period—one could find very striking examples even today—all sins against the sixth commandment are mortal sins (*in sexto mandato non datur parvitas materiae!*).[5] Conversely, all sins against the eighth commandment—which treats of truthfulness—are venial sins: lying as such is only a venial sin (*mendacium de se non est nisi leve peccatum!*).[6] Neither the rigor of the first sentence nor the laxity of the second has ever been convincingly demonstrated. They were frequently reiterated by the schoolmen, but fortunately were not taken as seriously by those actually engaged in the cure of souls. It is far from our intention to throw stones at the moral theologians, for in this matter all theologians live in glass houses, and for everyone to begin to throw stones at everybody else would be dangerous.

b. The second moment: unhistorical thinking in theology in general.[7] All too seldom in the last centuries have ecclesiastical formulations of doctrine been seen as historically conditioned, as dependent upon the concrete situation in the world, in the Church, in the theology of a particular time. According to a distinction of John XXIII we would say: in place of the "substance" of the faith (the faith itself), we became attached to the "vestments," the outer garments, the formulas of faith, and took them for the substance. In this way, the fragmentary character of all faith-knowledge which St. Paul stresses is overlooked: namely, that all our formulations of belief remain imperfect, incomplete, puzzling and fragmentary (cf. 1 Cor. 13:9–12). The result was that we had to take refuge in all kinds of clever distinctions, dialectical explanations—yes, even in not completely honorable theological tricks—in order to defend in doctrine what was not defensible, in order to avoid admitting that we had been wrong when mistakes were altogether possible and had in fact been made.

Interestingly enough, it is often the "ordinary" magisterial documents of the Church which cause difficulties for Catholic theologians, rather than those relatively few to which Catholic theology applies the highly questionable predicate "infallible." It is in theory self-evident that whatever is not infallible is fallible! But often this remained in the realm of theory: How much does it actually take before a Catholic theologian admits that a particular fallible pronouncement—like an encyclical or an address or a Roman decree —actually was in fact a mistake?

Is it not embarrassing to consider how long man's conscience was burdened in a completely incomprehensible way by erroneous doctrinal decisions with regard to the question of interest, of "usury"—a tragic affair which should serve to make contemporary moral theology more cautious in certain other questions;

Or how long Catholics were required, under threat of excommunication, to maintain the necessity of the Papal States;

Or how long it was before Galileo was removed from the Index (not until the nineteenth century—symbolic of the calamitous relationship between the Church and the natural sciences in the past centuries!);

Or how long it took before the translation of the canon of the Latin Mass, made at the beginning of the twentieth century, was released for the first time for approved use in the worship service;

Or how long it was before one might interpret the first three chapters of Genesis according to the results of modern science, and how much altogether unnecessary conflict transpired with condemnations, suppression of books and censorship: difficulties, first of all, regarding the six days of Creation in Genesis and the evolution of man, and finally, regarding original sin and polygenism in Genesis 3;

Or how few Catholic *exegetes* dare to express openly their opinion of the earlier decrees of the Papal Biblical Commission as seen in the light of contemporary research; how few Catholic *dogmatic theologians* venture to approach certain prickly questions in the history of dogma—in Christology, for example, or in the theology of the sacraments, or the theory of inspiration; or how few Catholic *moral theologians* risk giving unambiguous answers to certain burdensome questions of marriage morality?

Is it really so remarkable that the Catholic Church has been called, in malice, the "Church of truths" ("the true Church"), but the Protestant Church, the "Church of truthfulness"? This description is not fair on either side, but it contains some truth. Only after we have had to give way before the research of others, most reluctantly, with many "ifs" and "buts"; often only after a problem has become *passé* for the world, do we finally admit that we possibly —not certainly but perhaps—not exactly made a mistake, but were not entirely right.

Actually, one should not be too harsh with the moral theologians —or, for that matter, with theologians as a race. For, after all, hasn't the opinion been held quite generally in the Church—and often by laymen even more than theologians—that the Church could not under any circumstances openly admit that she had made a mistake? Our question is: Why was this opinion held? And this leads us to a third moment.

c. The third moment: a faulty image of the Church.[8]   There are two factors in this image of the Church. The first is the siege mentality. If a fortress is under attack in wartime, nothing—absolutely nothing—may be yielded to the enemy. One may not even open a window—the enemy must not see the conditions inside the fortress. That would be weakening, damaging: he would discover the best place to attack. The only possibilities are uncompromising resistance and unconditional defense: the doors and windows must be barricaded; morale kept up—the strong points stressed, the weak ones glossed over, the darker aspects of the situation painted white if possible—or at least gray.

One can understand, without necessarily excusing it, how this siege mentality came into being. It was established precisely at that moment when the Church was reconstructed as a centrally administered fortress, as a power institution, during the medieval investiture controversy of the popes against the emperors—a situation from which the Church derived both strength and weaknesses. This powerful institutional Church had to defend itself increasingly against attacks which often overshot the mark, attacks from without and within: against the rising national states and the medieval sects, against the Reformers, against Gallican and Jansenist, against the Enlightenment and the French Revolution, against the liberals, socialists, communists and fascists of the nineteenth and twentieth centuries. Nevertheless the situation in the Church with which we are concerned was in its elements already prepared before the high Middle Ages.

The other factor is the *ecclesiologia gloriae*: an ecclesiology of glory, of perfection, as opposed to an *ecclesiologia crucis,* an ecclesiology of the cross. Under the cross, the errors and sins of humanity, and of humanity in the Church, come to light; but by the false light of a premature glory there is ascribed to the Church here and now that which belongs only to the eschatological kingdom of God. This Church wants to be, here and now, the Church without spot or wrinkle—immaculate. This Church, although obviously made up of sinful and erring man, may not be called a sinful and erring community or Church. And so the earthly, pilgrim Church of man is increasingly transformed into a perfect heavenly being, one no longer under the necessity of praying out of the darkness of sin and error for the light of the Holy Spirit, but identifying itself more and more with the Holy Spirit of God and ascribing to itself, as far as possible, that which belongs to the Holy Spirit of God.

Such a Church had to make ever greater claims, claims which she herself was increasingly less able to justify. Such a Church had to parade her power before the world, rather than her weakness; had to boast of her rights, rather than her service. Such a Church found it difficult to come to grips with her errors and sins; she had to try to talk herself out of them. It must have been difficult for her to see herself as sincere and truthful. She must have become "a senate which does not make mistakes, and if it should, does not correct them, lest it should seem to have erred."

And when we look at all of this, the whole history of moral theology, of theology in general—yes, of the Church and the image of the Church: what was the result? We need not go into detail: Instead of accepting Christ, a large part of the world has rejected him because of the Church. Not only does the greater part of the world remain unconverted, but a large part of the Church herself has left this Church which could no longer be comprehended, in order to seek truthfulness outside her.

We do not want to dwell on this point, but one thing is certain: without an earnest conversion of the Church herself the situation will not improve. And we can say with joy that this conversion began decisively for the Catholic Church with the Second Vatican Council. This Church of Vatican II has renounced both the siege mentality and triumphalism. She sees herself once again as the people of God on pilgrimage, advancing through the darkness of bondage and error to the kingdom of God, in constant need of renewal until she is made perfect. An integral part of this renewal is that turning to a new truthfulness which has already been introduced by the Council and which has filled so many outside the Catholic Church as well as within it with new hope.[9] This truthfulness is, indeed, not new: it is the truthfulness of that message to which the Church appeals, which the gospel itself demands of the Church.

NOTES

1. Cf. B II below.
2. The statement is found in the introduction to his book *De Mendacio,* written in 395, where Augustine deals at length with the nature and malice of different forms of lying. Twenty-five years later he wrote yet another book, mainly against the Priscillians, who considered it lawful to conceal their heresy by lying (*Contra Mendacium,* about 420).
3. For Augustine (*De Mendacio* c. 3), a person is lying when he has in his mind something different from what he expresses in his words or in any kind of signs. A double, equivocal, false heart (*duplex cor*) or thinking

(*duplex cogitatio*) is typical of lying. Simply to say something false is not a lie: the person may be deceived. But if he has in his mind the desire to deceive the other person, if he wants to deceive the other with a false statement, then he is lying even if against his will he does in fact tell the truth. It is the *fallendi cupiditas* (or *voluntas fallendi*) which constitutes the sin (*culpa*) of lying. "Whether a person is a liar or not must be judged from his mind's utterance and not from the truth or falsehood of the things themselves."

4. Cf. *Summa Theologica* II-II, q. 110, a. 1.

5. So, for example, F. Hürth, *De Statibus* (Rome, 1946), p. 340: "All impure actions performed *with a lustful intention* are gravely sinful because of the intention from which they proceed." Likewise Bernard Häring, *Das Gesetz Christi* (Freiburg im Breisgau, 1952²), p. 1136; quoted from *The Law of Christ* (Westminster, Newman, 1966), Vol. 3, pp. 291-292, 695: "It is the teaching of most authors today that not only complete sexual satisfaction but also *every deliberate sexual gratification* outside well-ordered conjugal love is *a grave sin* if it is directly intended. Hence there is no slightness of matter (*parvitas materiae*) in any fully deliberate indulgence of sexual gratification." Häring thinks that "the objection that the rigor of this teaching concedes to the sixth commandment an unwarranted priority even over the great commandment of love can certainly not be sustained." As the only significant exceptions among Catholic moral theologians, he quotes Sanchez and—among more recent authors—A. Adam and J. Stelzenberger, who defends the thesis: "*Parvitas materiae* is possible according to the teaching of tradition."

6. So, for example, F. Hürth—P. M. Abellan, *De Praeceptis* II (Rome, 1948), p. 331: "A lie, whether verbal or real, of itself is not more than a *venial sin*. But if it is foreseen that as a result of it grave injury will be done to one's neighbor or if grave malice is involved from another source, it becomes mortal (*Summa Theologica* II-II, q. 110, aa. 3-4." Infidelity, too, is a venial sin in itself: "The same holds for not keeping *faith* (Acts 5:3; 1 Tim. 1:19; Rev. 21:10): of itself it is not more than a venial sin, but it can become mortal on account of some extrinsic reason." Häring, *op. cit.*, pp. 1285f. (English translation, pp. 563-4): "Most theologians of more recent times hold that a lie as untruth is only a venial sin. Obviously the venial sin may be rendered more gravely culpable through the motive or circumstances or some other reason, such as scandal." He quotes Mausbach in favor of the contrary opinion, at which "we should not take umbrage."

7. Cf. B VII below.

8. Cf. H. Küng, *The Church*, trans. Ray and Rosaleen Ockenden (New York, Sheed and Ward, 1968), A I, 2; II, 1; C III, 1.

9. Cf. B VI below.

III/Truthfulness as a Demand of the Message of Jesus

1. WHAT DID *Jesus* want? Jesus proclaimed the kingdom of God, which was near, which was even now beginning. Man must commit himself radically to God and his kingdom; must fulfil the will of God uncompromisingly in total love; must, because he is completely at God's disposal, be at the disposal of his fellow-man. In radical commitment to God the radical commitment to fellow-men! That was the message of Jesus, and it soon brought him a host of enemies. By its very demand for a human life lived in truth before God, it was a passionate protest against human dishonesty: a protest against the legalism of the man whose final norm is not the will of God and love, but an external law, a commandment; a protest against the feigned piety of a spiritless literalism and against an empty ritualism not in accord with the inner reality of the heart, striving for a merely external correctness rather than for the true and the genuine. Against this dishonesty, the gospel (Mt. 15:8f.; Mk. 7:6f.) quotes Isaiah (29:13), "This people honors me with their lips, but their heart is far from me; in vain do they worship me, teaching as doctrines the precepts of men." [1] What Christian could be so naive as to think that all this only applies to the Jews?

Jesus' protest is not merely against falsehood in the sense of a casuistic moral theology, but against everything which the gospels call "hypocrisy." The Greek word employed, *hypokrisis* or *hy-*

pokritai (-hypocrite), comes from *hypokrinesthai*. This is a familiar term of the Greek theater and means "to play a role." The verb is used for all play-acting, all hypocritical sham, which appears in a mask disguising its true nature and intentions—from God, from men, from itself. Jesus rebuked his contemporaries for this sham and hypocrisy—hypocrisy, as described in the Sermon on the Mount (Mt. 6:14, 5–8, 16–18), in almsgiving, at prayer, in fasting; but also hypocrisy in a dishonest casuistry: in connection with the Sabbath, for example, where Jesus must call attention to the obvious truth that "the sabbath was made for man, not man for the sabbath" (Mk. 2:27). Jesus says that prostitutes and publicans who are honest with themselves come off better than the so-called good people. As opposed to all dishonest legalism and pietism, it is love alone that is of final importance to Jesus: "Is it lawful on the sabbath to do good or to do harm, to save life or to kill?" (Mk. 3:4).

Can one imagine a sharper judgment on all dishonesty, falseness and hypocrisy than the great lamentation of Matthew 23, with its refrain, "you hypocrites"; "Woe to you, scribes and Pharisees, hypocrites! For you cleanse the outside of cup and of the plate, but inside they are full of extortion and rapacity. You blind Pharisee! first cleanse the inside of the cup and of the plate, that the outside also may be clean. Woe to you, scribes and Pharisees, hypocrites! for you are like whitewashed tombs, which outwardly appear beautiful, but within are full of dead men's bones and all uncleanness. So you also outwardly appear righteous to men, but within you are full of hypocrisy and iniquity." (Mt. 23: 25–28) But how encouraging for the truthful, honest and sincere man are the words "The eye is the lamp of the body. So, if your eye is sound, your whole body will be full of light; but if your eye is not sound, your whole body will be full of darkness." (Mt. 6:22f. par.)

2. But if we want to see what the message of Jesus means for the truthfulness of the *Church*, then we must not merely cite the statements of Jesus in the synoptic tradition against hypocrisy, but rather—as already indicated at the beginning of this section—start out from the *center of Jesus' message*. In her proclamation of

Jesus as the Christ, the Lord, the Church does indeed appeal at the same time to the message of Jesus itself. But this message of Jesus itself has for its theme, not the Church, but the reign of God. And this message of Jesus on God's reign is the radical question of the truthfulness of every Church which appeals to the message of Jesus. Compared to this radical question of the truthfulness of the Church, all other questions about the "institutional" factors are secondary.[2] Here the Church in her whole existence is involved and challenged. We shall try therefore to give concrete expression to this basic critical question from five aspects.[3]

a. A truthful Church, according to Jesus' message, is a *provisional* Church. Jesus proclaimed the reign of God as a decisively *future, end-time, final* event.

Question: Has the Church remained faithful to this message? does she regard herself really only as a *provisional* Church? More concretely: may a truthful Church in this end-time ever place herself at the center of her preaching? Must she not, arising as she does from the reign of God fulfilled in Christ, constantly point beyond herself to the reign of God which she awaits as the critical fulfilment of her mission? Is she not for the first time approaching not merely the particular but the universal, not merely the transitory but the definitive revelation of God's conquering glory? May she then ever set herself up as an end in herself, as if she could ever be a glory flourishing and complete in itself? As if men's decision were centered primarily not on God, not on Jesus the Christ, but on the Church. As if she were the end and fulfilment of world-history, as if she were the definitive reality. As if *her* definitions and declarations and not the word of the Lord remained for eternity. As if her institutions and constitutions and not the reign of God outlasted time. As if human beings existed for the Church and not the Church for human beings and just in this way for the reign of God.

Is not a Church which forgets in this end-time that she is something temporary, provisional, transitional, faced with excessive demands on her truthfulness? Must she not tire, relax her effort and break down, because she has no future? Is not that Church alone able to maintain her truthfulness which always remembers that she will find her goal, not in herself, but in God's kingdom? Because she thus knows that too much is not required of her, that she does not need to provide anything at all final, to offer any lasting home, that she must not be at all surprised if—in her provisional nature—she is shaken with doubts, blocked by hindrances and oppressed by cares? Does then the Church today really see herself in this way? So far as she can do so, she is a truthful Church.

b. According to the message of Jesus a truthful Church means an unassuming Church: Jesus proclaimed the reign of God as *a mighty deed of God himself.*

Question: has the Church remained faithful to this message? does this Church really see herself as an unassuming Church? More concretely: may a truthful Church in this end-time, while making the utmost exertions in the service of God's reign, ever want to create God's kingdom herself? As if God does not create it *for* her! As if she had to place her whole trust, not in his, but in her own action. Can the Church in this end-time do more than pray for God's reign, seek it, intensively prepare herself and the world by action and suffering for God's reign? May she ever glorify herself and boast before God and men of her own vital and formative power? May she ever raise claims against God by her resolutions, regulations and ideas, instead of defending God's claim in the world? Could she ever distrust the grace of God in her ecclesiastical omniscience and be intent on her home-made sovereignty and greatness? May she ever suppose that in fact she bestows grace herself, instead of being constantly in need of it? Has she not always to receive grace with empty hands, like a child, unassuming and trusting? Even when she fulfils her duty, must she not consider herself an unworthy servant?

Would not a Church be bound to become untruthful if she imagined that *she* creates what is decisive in this end-time, that she has to bring about, build up, erect the kingdom of God from her own resources and achievement? Would she not thus be bound to scatter and destroy, since she would lack selfless faith which trusts wholly in God's decisive deed? Is it not that Church alone which is convinced in trusting faith that God inaugurates, sustains and rules this end-time and that he will bestow the new, finished reality of the world and of men: is it not this Church alone which can be truthful and thus gather and build up, because power is granted to her humble trust? Since she then knows that, with all her efforts, what ultimately counts, is not *her* theories and practices, that it is not her catalogue of achievement and her brilliant statistics which guarantee the coming of the kingdom of God and hence that no want of an echo may prevent her from continuing to call, no failure dishearten her. Does then the Church today really see herself in this way? So far as she can do so, she is a truthful Church.

c. According to the message of Jesus a truthful Church means a *ministering* Church. Jesus preached the reign of God as a *purely religious* reign.

Question: Has the Church remained faithful to this message? does this Church really see herself as a *ministering* Church? More concretely: May a truthful Church in this end-time ever act like a religious-political theocracy? Is her character not that of a spiritual diaconia? Instead of setting up an empire of spiritual-unspiritual power, has she not been given the grace of ministry in the form of a servant: service of God as service of men and service of men as service of God? How could she then in this end-time ever have recourse to the methods of secular seizure and establishment of power, of political strategy and intrigue? How could she radiate worldly glory and splendor, how assign places of honor to right and left, how hand out titles and distinctions of worldly dignity? How could she want to hoard the goods of this world, money and gold, to keep more than is necessary? How could she get mixed up with the powers of this world, how simply identify herself with any sort of worldly grouping, a political party, a cultural association, an economic and social power-group? How commit herself uncritically and unconditionally to a particular economic, social, cultural, political, philosophical, ideological system? How could she fail constantly to disturb, estrange, question these worldly powers and systems with her revolutionary message and precisely thus then also have to face their resistance and attack? How could she avoid suffering, contempt, calumny, persecution? How could she want to make a triumphal procession instead of a way of the cross? How could she thus ever regard outsiders as her enemies to be hated and destroyed and not rather as neighbors to be embraced with understanding and helpful love?

Does a Church which in this end-time overlooks the fact that she exists for selfless service to men, to enemies, to the world, not lose her truthfulness and thus also her dignity, her validity, her reason for existing, because she abandons the true imitation of Christ? Conversely, does not the Church alone which remains aware of the fact that it is not she, but God's reign, which will come "in power and glory": does not this Church alone find her true greatness and thus her truthful existence only in being small? Because she then knows that she is great precisely without the show of power and splendor, that she can rely upon the agreement and support of the mighty ones of this world only very conditionally and to a limited extent; that her existence is constantly ignored, neglected and merely tolerated by the world or even regretted, deplored and wished away; that her activity is constantly ridiculed, suspected, disapproved and hindered; that for her nevertheless, above all other dominations, God's reign is unassailable. Does the Church today really see herself in this way? So far as she can do so, she is a truthful Church.

d. According to the message of Jesus, a truthful Church is a Church *conscious of guilt*. Jesus proclaimed the reign of God as a saving event for *sinners*.

Question: Has the Church remained faithful to this message? Does this Church really see herself as a Church *conscious of guilt?* More concretely: may a truthful Church in this end-time—for all her opposition to the world and its powers—ever behave as a threatening, intimidating institution, preaching doom and creating fear? May she announce to the world tidings of doom instead of the message of salvation, threatening words instead of the message of joy, a declaration of war instead of the message of peace? The Church exists in fact not for the pious and just, but for the unjust and the impious. She should in fact not condemn and anathematize, but—for all the seriousness of her message—heal, pardon and save. Even her often unavoidable admonitions should in fact never be ends in themselves, but pointers to God's offer of grace. Nor can she—even with all the proofs of grace reaching her and precisely because of these proofs—in fact ever give herself airs as a self-righteous caste or class of the pure and holy. She can in fact never imagine evil, unholiness, impurity as existing only outside herself. There is in fact nothing within her that is perfect—not in peril, not fragile, not dubious—that does not need to be constantly corrected and excelled. The front line between the world and the reign of God runs in fact right through the Church, right through the heart of the individual member of the Church.

Will not a Church which in this end-time does not want to know that she exists as composed of sinful men for sinful men not become hard-hearted, self-righteous, merciless and thus untruthful? Does she thus still deserve God's mercy and men's trust? Is this truthfulness, holiness and justice, which she herself cannot produce, not a gift of grace solely to that Church which gives full weight to the fact that only the consummated reign of God will have wheat and tares, good and bad fish, separated from one another? Since such a Church then knows that she does not need to adopt a high moral tone in the world, as if with her everything were ordered for the best, that she carries her treasures in only earthen vessels, that her lights are faint and flickering, her faith weak, her knowledge obscure and her confession stammered out, that there is not a single sin or lapse which cannot become a temptation to her and to which she is not already exposed in one way or another, that—for all her constant dissociation from sin—she can never have an excuse for dissociating herself from sinners? Does the Church then today really see herself in this way? So far as she can do so, she is a truthful Church.

e. According to the message of Jesus, a truthful Church is an *obedient* Church. Jesus demanded for the reign of God *man's radical decision for God*.

Question: Has the Church remained faithful to this message? Does the Church really see herself as an *obedient* Church? Is not the truthful Church—and particularly as such—also faced with the choice: God and his reign or the world and its reign? Must not she also allow nothing to hold her back from a radical decision for God? Must not she in particular constantly turn to *metanoia*, away from the wickedness of the world, and submit herself to the coming reign of God, so that from this position she can turn in love to the world and to men: not therefore in ascetic separation from the world, but in radical loving obedience to God's will in the ordinary affairs of the world; not in flight from the world, but in working in the world?

Can the Church ever be allowed to avoid this radical obedience to God's will? As if perhaps the demands of the gospel held only for the "wicked world" and not also for the constantly resecularized Church. As if the Church could discharge her obligation of obedience to God's holy will by obedience to herself. As if she could issue her own liturgical, dogmatic and juridical laws and regulations, traditions and customs as commandments of God; as if she could place them above or even alongside God's will as it became known in Jesus Christ. As if she could declare as eternal laws what are always time-conditioned arrangements and which can then be adapted to the ever recurring present only with the aid of artificial and twisted interpretation. As if in matters of decisive importance she could "swallow a camel" and on the other hand with petty casuistry "strain at a gnat." As if she could thus lay on men's shoulders the burden of innumerable laws and regulations which they are not able to bear. As if, instead of a heartfelt obedience out of love for God, she could demand a blind obedience out of fear: the obedience of someone who does not act in this way because he understands and approves the requirement, but only because it is commanded, and would act otherwise if it were not commanded. As if there could be a question here of external legality instead of internal conviction, of the "traditions of the elders" instead of the "signs of the times," of lip-service instead of sincerity of heart, of "commandments of men" instead of the absolute, limitless will of God.

Does not a Church place herself in chains, does she not enslave herself, does she not become untruthful, if she forgets in this present age whom she has to obey, if she seizes dominion for herself, makes herself sovereign, sets herself up as mistress? Conversely, does not that Church alone become truthful and free which—for all her failures—is constantly intent upon God's reign and remembers to whom she belongs, for whom she has to decide, for whom she must constantly decide afresh without compromise and without reserve? Does not such an obedient Church become truly free to imitate Christ's ministry to the world; free for the service of God, in which she serves men, free for the service of men in which she serves God; free to overcome the body, sin and death, through the cross of the Risen One; free for the all-embracing creative love which changes and renews the world; free for an unshakable active hope for the coming kingdom of God of complete justice, of eternal life, of true freedom and of cosmic peace, for the final reconciliation of mankind with God and the removal of all impiety? Does the Church then today really see herself in this way? So far as she can do so, she is a truthful Church.

3. This is what Jesus' message means for the Church and her truthfulness. We were merely raising questions, we were raising them as members of this Church and precisely *in* the Church we have more right than we would have outside her to raise these questions openly and honestly. Questions which undoubtedly are also indictments. Questions which undoubtedly are not merely indictments. This is precisely what is so difficult about these questions: they cannot simply be answered with a smooth "Yes" or "No." The reality of the Church as such is too complex for this, too manifold, too much light and shade, nature and un-nature. In theological terms: the concrete Church is the Church of God and at the same time—with all her institutions and constitutions— Church of men, of sinful men constantly betraying the gospel afresh; she is at the same time in every individual member and in every one of her institutions both truthful and untruthful Church, but not each as balanced off against the other or in the same way.

In Jesus Christ—who, from Jesus preaching, has become through his death and his new life in God the Christ who is preached and thus made possible at all the new reality of the

Church—this holds: untruthfulness is the Church's past; truthfulness her future. Each is present in its own way: the past as past, as the old; the future as future, as the new. The past of untruthfulness has no longer a future for the Church at present, but it remains her own past. The Church has been rescued from untruthfulness, but she still remains under attack. The Church therefore must constantly turn away again from her past towards her future, which is her truthfulness. This future by God's grace is already bestowed on her as a pledge, she is wholly and entirely determined by it. But she must constantly seize it afresh, have it given to her. Because she is truthful, she ought also to be truthful: the indicative demands the imperative. This is what the apostolic preaching requires.

The New Testament is concerned with the idea of truth at every turn; it is one of the basic concepts of the New Testament. Reflecting the sense of the Old Testament word *emet,* the Greek word *aletheia,* truth, is used in the New Testament to mean that which is certain and valid, the binding norm; in other words, that on which one may rely. In the New Testament, "truth" also has the Greek meaning of conclusive evidence, manifest reality, and, consequently, the correct doctrine. St. Paul simply calls his entire apostolic activity "the open statement of the truth" (2 Cor. 4:2). The preaching of the gospel can be called "truthful speech" (2 Cor. 6:7; Col. 1:5; Eph. 1:13). The Christian faith is (1 Pet. 1:22) "obedience to the truth" (cf. Gal. 5:7).

But it is St. John who has given the word "truth" its deepest meaning. For him it is the opposite of falsehood. Falsehood is not understood in the casuistic sense, however, but rather as designating the essence of that human world, given over to death, removed from God, which, shutting itself off from the light, tries to set itself free from its Creator and falls into the abyss of self-deception.

Jesus came into the world as the light, to bear witness to the truth (18:37); grace and truth came through him (1:17) and the knowledge of the truth is promised to those who believe in him (8:32). The word that Jesus brings is truth (17:17); yes, he is himself the truth (14:6). By "truth" John never means a simple statement or a teaching, not even reality in opposition to deception. He means, rather, that reality which is the only genuinely true reality: the reality proper to God. This truth "speaks," reveals Jesus (8:45); his Spirit leads one into this truth (16:3), not simply into a new teaching or doctrine or theology about God, in the newly evident reality of God, as it reveals itself in Jesus (14:9–11). This is the truth which sets us free (8:32). A new existence, a new life, a new birth of man "out of God," springing from this truth, this reality of God himself is actually possible.

Now we see: human truthfulness, according to the New Testament, is basically nothing other than the ethical demand which follows as an altogether obvious imperative from the new reality: To live in God's truth or reality demands truthfulness of a man. The realization of this truthfulness, however, depends upon the gift of God's grace. Left on his own, he falls again and again into dishonesty. But he may overcome his insufficiency and guilt in asking for the gift of truthfulness.

The language of the New Testament is rich in examples of the interrelation of truth and truthfulness: the common Greek word *aletheia,* as well as the Old Testament word *emet,* means both truth and truthfulness: that which may be relied upon, dependability, sincerity, honesty (cf. 2 Cor. 7:14; 11:10; 1 Cor. 5:8; Phil. 1:18; 1 Tim. 2:7). In the same way, the related adjectives *alethes* (cf. Mk. 12:14; 2 Cor. 6:8; Rom. 3:4; Jn. 3:33; 7:18; 8:26) and *alethinos* mean both "true" *and* "truthful." Truthfulness is so much taken for granted that it receives little attention in the paranese (cf. Mt. 5:37; Eph. 4:15; 22–25; Phil. 4:8). However, the New Testament condemns almost no other sin as vehemently as hypocrisy (cf. Mt. 6:1–17; 15:7f.; 23; Acts 5:1–11; 1 Tim. 4:1f.). We hardly need to be reminded that Paul opposed Peter to his face because he had "played it false" and his conduct "did not square with the truth of the Gospel" (cf. Gal. 2:11–14). Significant in this regard is the weight which the New Testament places upon the *parresia* (originally meaning the right to speak of everything): that is, upon candor before God and man, not obscuring or hushing up anything, unembarrassedly frank, utterly fearless.

In contrast to textbook theology, a close relationship between truth and truthfulness is found not only in the biblical view but also in that of the modern world. We can see once again that there is no fundamental contradiction between the view of the modern world which looks to the future and that of the original biblical message which looks to the past, or between *aggiornamento* and reform; we can see once again that it is not the clear, original biblical message itself, but rather the ecclesiastical innovations of the eleventh, thirteenth, sixteenth or nineteenth centuries which no longer matter to the modern world; which are—with some justice —reckoned as belonging to the *ancien régime*. In the final analysis, also, the modern world does not care, as far as the human-personal sphere is concerned, for abstract, purely "objective" truths. Truth, for the modern world, does not simply consist in the intellect's abstract and neutral conformity with the object (*adaequatio intellectus et rei*). Finally, only those truths which are apprehended, realized and lived existentially are relevant for the modern world. Engagement is demanded, the unconditional, unreserved commitment to the truth; not an unconcerned, theorizing attitude of the mere observer. The only thing that counts, says Sartre, is total commitment.[4]

In this way, also for the modern world, truth is bound to man's personal existence—that is, to his truthfulness. Veracity is the *conditio sine qua non* of truth. Only in truthfulness is the truth of the person revealed. Only the honest man is disposed to apprehend the truth which sustains him. The full truth is closed to those who are dishonest with themselves. In this sense truthfulness is much more basic than truth itself. Even those who cannot agree on truth must nevertheless agree on truthfulness. Honesty makes dialogue possible. For those living in a pluralistic society, it is not truth but honesty, truthfulness, which is the basis of all tolerance and of all social life and co-operation. Thus does honesty become a basic ethical demand, touching everyone and everything concerning man's relationship to himself, to society and to God.

NOTES

1. All scriptural passages are quoted from *The Holy Bible, Revised Standard Version* (New York, Nelson, 1946, 1952). Copyrighted 1946 and 1952 by the Division of Christian Education of the National Council of Churches.
2. This too must be noted. Cf. below B IV-V.
3. The discussion here follows closely the much more far-reaching and reasoned exposition on the message of Jesus in my book, *The Church* B. The arguments there set out must be applied to the problem of the Church's truthfulness and we do not hesitate to repeat verbally some of the statements on the message of Jesus, since they appear to us to be so fundamental. (I have translated afresh several pages in the author's German, but inevitably there are a number of close but unintended resemblances between these and the pages in the other book. Trans.)
4. J.-P. Sartre, *L'Existentialisme est un humanisme,* Paris, 1946.

IV/The Consequences for the Future

HOW CAN the truth be found, asks modern man, among those who do not live in the light of truth? What does this mean for the Church, so vulnerable, despite all her talk about "truth," to the objection that she lacks veracity? It is absolutely clear: the Church is challenged by the message of Jesus himself, by the whole apostolic witness and by the modern world as well, which thirsts for genuine truthfulness; is challenged to a renewed, bold and joyful honesty. What does this imply for the concrete life of the Church, first negatively, then positively?

a. As long as the Church is guided by the biblical witness, she will be safeguarded against *false candor*—something which is a real possibility. There is one danger to which Protestant Churches and Protestant theology seem peculiarly liable; for if Catholics have repeatedly ridden the idea of truth into the ground through proclaiming and defending it dishonestly, Protestant Churches have often carried truthfulness—personal conviction, conscience—to ridiculous extremes in making it absolute, so that in the end it was isolated and dissociated from all truth, from the reality which it should express. The neglect of truthfulness leads to hypocrisy, but the exaggeration of truthfulness leads to destructive fanaticism. Of course a Christian must never lie or be hypocritical or deceive himself, his fellow-man or God. But the person who is a fanatic

43

for honesty and freedom of conscience thinks he has the right to say anything at any time to anyone—yes, and even the obligation to do so.

He has no sense of that discretion which never exposes oneself or others unnecessarily.

He intentionally sets aside his responsibility to his neighbor and the community in favor of his veracity.

He does not take into consideration the concrete situation of his fellow-man, or the community, or the Church, a situation which may call for reserve rather than stubborn intrusion.

He believes he has the right to hurt and wrong others in the name of honesty.

Above all, because of his personal truthfulness and good conscience, he thinks he is always in the right and need not even consider the possibility of being wrong; he is protected from all dangers, having a charm, so to speak, against caprice. Thus the man who is fanatical about honesty falls into loveless self-righteousness and subjective dogmatism. More and more he dissociates himself from the truth, from the reality which is to be expressed and which his honesty should always serve. The effects upon himself and the community are inevitably destructive.

Indeed there is, as Augustine says, a "veritas homicida," a murderous truth; and there is an honesty which Bonhoeffer calls "Satanic truth," one which callously sacrifices the common good and the welfare of other people. Particularly among Protestants, this kind of fanaticism of the honest conscience has done great damage to the Church, especially when theologians, even with the best intentions, have concerned themselves all too little with the Church and her unity, the common faith and their own relationship to that faith. There are so many people who are in good conscience *and* are very, very wrong. We must not today, in our zeal for reform, imitate the *mistakes* of the Protestant Reformation. If Catholic theology can learn greater veracity from the Protestants, so also can the Protestants acquire from the Catholics a greater sense of responsibility for the community of the Church and her unity, a more intimate association with it and a more concrete commitment to it.[1]

For the Christian trying to live according to the New Testament teaching, truthfulness cannot be the one and only virtue: without it, to be sure, no other virtue is true and unadulterated, but unless truthfulness is seen and experienced in relation to all other basic human principles—justice, prudence, etc.—it will itself be adulterated. How truthfulness and the concrete virtues are to be combined in a concrete case is something that cannot be decided on the basis of a general principle: it is a matter for individual decision in the concrete situation. However, truthfulness will above all be adulterated if it is not guided in every instance by love, which alone can show it "the best way of all." Only if it is continuously revitalized by love can truthfulness be detached from the rigor and coldness peculiar to it in isolation. Love frees truthfulness from that egotistical arbitrariness, arrogance and hair-splitting which not only severs it from the truth it must serve but destroys it. Love warms and illuminates honesty, opens it wholly to the truth it should reveal for the sake of serving one's fellow-man, and so one's God: "Be renewed in the spirit of your minds, and put on the new nature, created after the likeness of God in true righteousness and holiness. Therefore, putting away falsehood, let every one speak the truth with his neighbor, for we are members of one another." (Eph. 4:23–25)

b. This genuinely Christian truthfulness is demanded of the Church categorically; it is a task with which the Church is never done. Having no guarantee against dishonesty, the Church must continually accept truthfulness as a gift of God's grace in order to take hold of it ever anew. What matters here in a positive way for the post-conciliar Church is *the courage to act!*

If especially the post-conciliar Catholic Church wants to convince the world, beyond any doubt, that she is truthful, honorable, sincere, decent—and therefore credible—it is not enough for her to ponder, express, decree and promulgate truths, she must bring these truths to a genuine realization; she must commit herself unconditionally, unmistakably, clearly and unreservedly to the truth. The world today is not especially interested in grandiose ecclesiastical theories about the world and its progress, whether they pertain to yesterday's pessimistic declamations or today's optimistic declarations. The modern world is moving ahead—and in great part in spite of the Church. And the modern world will continue to move ahead—with, without, or against the Church. What the modern world expects of the Church—especially since the closing of the Second Vatican Council—are concrete decisions. General principles are important, practical imperatives more important, actual results most important of all. We must achieve results.

Today the Church is in possession of fascinating possibilities for a bold, constructive, and hopeful realization of Christian truthfulness. Here we merely sketch a few of the concrete possibilities, all of which are definitely in line with the objectives of the Second Vatican Council:

Truthfulness basically in *preaching the Gospel:*
Our preaching, from having been a lame, emotionally distorted moralism or a barren, alienated dogmatism (or simply a request for more money!), should once again flow from the original message of Christ and thus, openly and fearlessly, come to grips with the real needs and problems of modern man and his faith today.

Truthfulness in *theology in general:*
Instead of muffling the discussion of unpleasant questions by authoritarian measures, we should go to the root of these very problems in full Christian candor. They are difficult and dangerous, to be sure, but in many instances they hold the keys to the future. We should become more practised in theological truthfulness through courageous and frank theological thought, discourses, discussions, and publications. And to that end, we should resolutely discard the last remnants of the earlier, absolutist policy of censorship in the Catholic Church. After the fortunate abolition of certain inquisitional proceedings and of the Index by Paul VI, we

should also do away with the discreditable and authoritarian censoring of theological books before publication—a practice first introduced by Alexander VI—according to the standards of which presumably not even St. Paul's epistles—in many places all to "radical," "one-sided," "polemical," "inopportune"—could have been published.

Truthfulness in *exegesis and systematic theology:*

Rather than trying to cover up new problems with patent solutions and outworn dogmatic formulas, we should produce a new answer from the original Christian message for a new time, employing a worthy exegetical, historical and systematic method. We should thus be decisively casting off an outmoded world view in order that the original message should be clear for the contemporary world. We should tolerate the tensions, inconsistencies and contradictions within ecclesiastical traditions and the history of dogma without trying to reconcile them by resorting to ingenious tricks; thus we shall allow the gospel itself to sift out the good seed and make it fruitful.

Truthfulness in *moral teaching:*

Rather than confining ourselves to speaking about love and marriage with great depth and beauty, we should free ourselves from time-worn answers and provide an accurate, honest and reasonable solution to the difficult problems of marriage morality, especially that of birth control: an answer which places the responsibility for an honest moral decision on the parents and leaves all methodological questions to the competent specialist.

Truthfulness in *ecumenical relations:*

Rather than engaging in a lot of talk about ecumenical convictions, we should take concrete steps towards mutual understanding, and this means especially that we should recognize—as we did before 1918—the validity of the hundreds of thousands of mixed marriages arbitrarily declared invalid since the publication of the new Code of Canon Law, and we should devise a regulation for marriage, baptism and religious education which excludes all violation of conscience.

Truthfulness in the *Church press:*
Instead of exhorting the secular press to greater truthfulness, we should avoid, in the Church herself, triumphal reports of our work and one-sided statistics. We should report our failures, too, and let our opponents express their views completely, objectively and with greater justice.

Truthfulness in ecclesiastical *dress* and *ceremonial:*
Rather than only talking about the "Church of the Poor," we should simply begin—courageously and without romanticism—to rid ourselves of the out-of-date and often ridiculous clerical pomp and circumstance in both liturgy and life. And rather than only talking about evangelical simplicity, we should quietly and peacefully bury, with—perhaps—a few sentimental tears, the feudal titles and salutations, decorations and honors, gestures and customs which the world has long since found curious.

Truthfulness in the *education of the clergy:*
Rather than merely encouraging vocations to fill our seminaries, we should make a place in them for fresh air and openness to the world, contemporary educational methods and human freedom (especially in regard to the law of celibacy).

Truthfulness in the *administration of the Church:*
Rather than always boasting of our catholicity, we should provide for a just representation of the different nationalities *and* the different mentalities in the central administration of the Church at Rome, thereby permitting a somewhat more professional competence to come to the fore, and a theology which is *au courant*. A more radical reform of the Roman Curia remains the critical problem of the post-conciliar Church.

Truthfulness in *relation to the world:*
Instead of always calling attention only to our progress and or-

ganic development to an ever greater perfection, we should quietly
and modestly acknowledge the wrong we have done and our stupid
mistakes, without glossing over or qualification, thereby moving
towards improvement and renewal.

One could easily go on. But I want to challenge *you* to go on—
not in theoretical itemizing but in practical accomplishments! It
depends on you to what extent truthfulness illuminates the Church
—your Church and the whole of Christendom. To what kind of
Christian, to what kind of Church, does the future belong?

Not to a Church which is lazy, shallow, indifferent, timid and
weak in its faith;

Not to a Church which expects blind obedience and fanatical
party loyalty;

Not to a Church which is the slave of its own history, always putting on the brakes, suspiciously defensive and yet, in the end,
forced into agreement;

Not to a Church which is anti-critical, practically anti-intellec-
tual and dilettantish;

Not to a Church which is blind to problems, suspicious of empir-
ical knowledge, yet claiming competent authority for everyone and
everything;

Not to a Church which is quarrelsome, impatient and unfair in
dialogue;

Not to a Church which is closed to the real world.

In short: the future does not belong to a Church which is dishonest!

No, the future belongs:

To a Church which knows what it does not know;

To a Church which relies upon God's grace and wisdom, and
has in its weakness and ignorance a radical confidence in God;

To a Church which is strong in faith, joyous and certain, yet
self-critical;

To a Church filled with intellectual desire, spontaneity, anima-
tion and fruitfulness;

To a Church which has the courage of initiative, and the courage to take risks;

To a Church which is altogether open to the real world;

In short: the future belongs to a thoroughly truthful Church!

NOTES

1. Cf. below B III.

I/A Challenge to the Church

THIS BOOK is not an answer to my friend Charles Davis, England's leading Catholic theologian, who left the Church in December 1966. The first, basic part of this book (that is, A), anticipating many of Davis' questions in regard to truth and truthfulness and—apart from some additions on the message of Jesus (in A III)—here reproduced unaltered, was completed for my lectures in the United States a couple of months before Davis' sensational step. This chapter contains merely the brief analysis, provisionally sifting out the essential points, which I wrote down soon after Davis had published an account of the reasons for his action in the London Sunday newspaper *The Observer* on January 1, 1967. Now that I have read Davis' fuller justification, which appeared later in the same year,[1] I feel that it confirms my analysis. With a few points clarified, it may therefore be regarded as an introduction and transition to the second part (B), in order to show quite concretely how the question of truth and truthfulness reaches to the roots of the existence both of the Church as a whole and of her members as individuals.

There are numerous reasons which can lead a person to leave the Church. Some are not genuine. Departures from the Church for selfish motives (lack of moral restraint, neglect of God's commandments, contempt for essential rules of the ecclesial community) are painful for the Church, but not of much interest.

51

These reasons do not apply to the departure of Charles Davis, the English theologian, professor of dogmatics at Heythrop College, Editor of the semi-official *Clergy Review,* member of the editorial board of the international theological review *Concilium,* Cardinal Heenan's theologian at the Council and pillar of the renewal of the Church in England. As an act of truthfulness it must be taken seriously in the Church.

No departure from the Church in recent decades has had such an international impact, inside and outside the Catholic Church. For England it means what the departure of Karl Rahner would have meant for Germany or of Yves Congar for France—although the English theologian scarcely carries the same weight as they do. Impossible to ignore it, suppress it, say nothing about it. This departure from the Church is significant—and largely significant as providing a model, a pattern—for the whole Church: as—in the opposite direction—was the conversion in the last century of another theologian, John Henry Newman. Therefore it has to be discussed.

Davis—as he had every right to do—announced his action publicly in the press. It would in any case have become a matter of public interest. Or ought Davis to have left it to others to talk, puzzle, reflect—or be silent—about his motives? No: it is a matter of urgency to hear Davis' reasons, to examine them critically, but not in a hasty, superficial way. Absolute truthfulness is inescapable when judging the motives of a man who left the Church for the sake of truthfulness. Slick answers, rendering the problem innocuous, are of help neither to Davis nor to the Church. And there were a variety of cheap reactions to Davis' departure.

Cherchez la femme. This is a natural and yet facile reaction. At the same time as he made known his departure from the Church, Charles Davis was frank enough to declare his intention to marry: without a woman's helpful love, under the pressure of the ecclesiastical system, he would probably have had a nervous breakdown within a few years; psychologically it would scarcely have been possible to break with this system, with which he had been most intimately associated for so long during his whole life and activity. This he says himself in the *Observer* article, in which he expounds his motives in all honesty. As a result of various immediate reactions, Charles Davis assumes that some who might have understood his leaving the Church cannot understand or pardon his marriage. Frankly speaking, I am not one of these. And yet I would have preferred the departure from the Church and the marriage not to have been linked together in this way: for the sake of the force and the unalloyed clarity of his protest.

We may distinguish two hypotheses.

First of all, if Davis, the Catholic priest, had married without leaving the Church at the same time, this would have been understood as at least an indirect, pointed, unambiguous protest: a protest against the law (not the charism!) of celibacy for priests (no longer for deacons!) within the Latin (not the whole Catholic!) Church. It would not have been possible in the Church *a priori* to deny any justification to such a protest: not only because, since the Council—and even particularly in the Anglo-Saxon countries— priests and laymen in surprisingly increasing numbers are demanding the repeal of the law of celibacy (alarming too the rapidity of the increase in the number of those who have given up their priestly office for this reason); not only because in modern society a law of celibacy becomes more and more problematic; but also and fundamentally because such a law can scarcely be justified from the New Testament message, which assures to *every* Christian full liberty in regard to marriage and celibacy.[2]

The opposite hypothesis would be that Davis, the theologian, had left the Church without marrying at once. This, too, would have been understood as a strong, unambiguous protest: a protest against the Roman system as Davis feels it, its lack of freedom, its dishonesty, its inhumanity. Here too, there could have been no *a priori* denial in the Church of any justification for such a protest: for Davis' arguments—and the whole discussion confirms this—indisputably point to open wounds in the Church.

But now Davis has done both at one and the same time. That is his responsibility. But the mingling of the two robs his protest of the clarity it would otherwise have had. There are those now who dispense themselves from reflecting on the departure from the Church, because they explain it by pointing to the simultaneous marriage. This is wrong, unjust.

We know that his wife did not talk him into this decision, in fact that she was not informed from the beginning about the final choice. Yet he could rely upon her agreeing with him and joining him with absolute certainty. This is important for our judgment. According to his own statement, it was only a woman's love which gave him strength to leave the Church. A question arises: Would he perhaps have remained in the Church if this woman—on whose motives we certainly do not wish to place a false construction— had applied all her resources from the very beginning to make it possible for Charles Davis freely and honorably to remain in the Church in spite of all difficulties? [3]

The responsibility of that American theological student in this matter is therefore by no means slight: for her and for Charles Davis we can only hope frankly that they have not taken too great a burden on themselves. But, in spite of the unfortunate mingling of motives, *cherchez la femme* is not the answer in this case. It would in fact be a lame excuse if at the same time Davis' theological-ecclesial reasons were not taken wholly and entirely seriously. And these reasons—it must even now be admitted—are so weighty that, by comparison, Davis' marriage is relatively unimportant. Had it not been for the force of these arguments, it would have been easy in these days for Davis to be released from the law of celibacy in order then to continue his theological work at peace with the Church as a lay theologian. The fact that he did not choose this—although certainly the easier way—proves clearly that for him some other factor was decisive.

"Let us pray for him": this reaction too, however appropriate, may be inadequate. It must certainly be recognized as a fine gesture of tolerance and good will that Davis' bishop, when making a public statement of his position, insisted that his conscience and his personal relationships were Davis' own affair: the best way of proving his friendship for Davis could only be by praying that God would guide him in all that he undertook. A less magnanimous bishop would certainly have issued a public condemnation of Davis. The acting editor-in-chief of the *Osservatore Romano* also quoted this response with approval in an article on Davis.

In trying to make an objective analysis of Davis' action, we must then leave open the question of whether he would have left the Church, even if he had not got to know a woman who would have influenced him decisively in the opposite direction; but in that case the other question—just as important with reference to Davis and the heavy responsibility of bishops towards theologians —must not be suppressed. As long as we in the Church do not summon up the honesty and civil courage to criticize loyally, but publicly, not only the Roman Curia (as is the universal custom today), but also the local pastors when they have publicly failed in their service to the Church, there will scarcely be a fundamental renewal in the institutional Church of the different countries.

We spoke of the bishop's generous response, of his respect for Davis' conscientious decision. But would a theologian who complains so bitterly of the institutional Church, of the hierarchy, have left the Church even if in his bishop he had found a real friend? A bishop, that is—and there are many examples of such today—who has a deep understanding for the pressing responsibility and the numerous anxieties of a theologian at the front; who has acquired a more than average insight into the problems, methods and solutions of modern theology without wanting just for that reason to be considered a theological expert; who helps his theologian where he can, protects him wherever it is necessary, discusses and works with him as often as the opportunity arises, in order to contribute to the necessary interchange of theory and practice, scholarship and pastoral care; who thus appears in every way, not as the representative of the machinery of power and of a rigid ecclesiastical system, but as a credible witness of the gospel of that Jesus who gave himself for men and for their afflictions even at the point where it goes against the self-made laws and theories of the "system."

What does all this mean? In this connection what is decisive is not the personal aspect, but the universally important. Here, simply

to pray for the other person does not settle the matter. This holds
especially for pastors, for *all* pastors serving in the government of
the Church. For all the outward signs of friendliness and the "new
style" of bishops, how many priests are nevertheless heard today
on all sides complaining of authoritarian, negative, unintelligent
treatment by their bishops? How often—in spite of astute ecclesiastical policy and administration—do they miss the true spirit of the
liberating gospel? How much inward dissatisfaction, how much
mistrust and pent-up emotion, how much discouragement—even
despair—among the pastoral clergy have their roots here?

All this too is not accusation but questioning. Ought we not to begin first of all with prayer for ourselves, for God to show *us* our way,
open *our* eyes to our own defects and to what we might do better in
accordance with the true message of Jesus Christ? Hence our
prayer must not be for that poor publican there, but "for us poor
sinners." And from this prayer, in which the other person is included, must emerge the recognition of our guilt and of the frequent failure of our system, and hence the bold resolution for
personal *metanoia*, to change our ideas and be converted, to reform the system and the Church's government in accordance with
the gospel of Jesus Christ himself. From the humble *oratio* there
must proceed the self-critical *actio* on oneself and on the ecclesiastical system. From reflective reform, renewal! We must not merely
complain of the situation in the Church, but—in the sphere of
life, small or great, in which we are competent—alter it! This is
applied truthfulness.

"A typically English affair." This too is a natural and yet—in the
last resort—again a cheap reaction. In this connection there can be
no question of going into the very complex situation of the Catholic
Church in England and its difficulties, its strength and weakness,
its centuries-long oppression by the English state, the ghetto situation and the minority mentality arising out of this, the social and
cultural position of inferiority, the concentration on making converts; furthermore, the apologetic-defensive consolidation in post-
Tridentine theology and piety which was shattered only by the

Council, the Irish influence in people and episcopate, the cleavage between the bishops formed in Rome in the Roman way and the Catholic intellectuals educated in the English universities in an English way. All this would need a more differentiated presentation by a more competent author, and my English friends will understand that I am not making any judgments on these things.

They might naturally raise the analogous question as to whether Davis would have taken the same step in a country with a less solid "Catholicism." The more solid this Catholicism, the less hope of a radical renewal, the greater the temptation to seek a solution outside it. And it may not have been entirely by chance that Charles Davis decided on his action in the midst of preparing for the meeting of an official study-commission of Catholics and Anglicans, without on that account (and this is significant) becoming an Anglican.

Yet Davis himself has explained that it was not the situation in England which decisively influenced him in leaving the Church. In this we must believe him. Therefore we should not be looking for a feeble alibi. Rather is it of fundamental importance to appreciate the fact that the questions raised by Davis are not merely specifically English, but general Catholic questions. We may recall these.

Does the contemporary institutional Church, with its large claims, really have behind it the biblical message to which it appeals? Is it really what Jesus wanted or only the degenerate form of a community which originally had quite a different structure? What are we to make of the development of its teaching, its dogmas? is this really an organic development or a history of contradictions, frequently tidied up? What is the basis of the new Marian dogmas and have the modern papal claims—primacy and infallibility—the original message of Christ behind them? How does the Church's magisterium function in practice? Does it help men or does it sacrifice men in their concrete need (birth control!) to principles laid down by itself? How much honesty and straightforwardness is there in the Church? Can a theologian in the concrete Church really be creatively active in freedom and intellectual integrity? and so on.

Read once again, sentence for sentence, Davis' justification in the *Observer,* or now also in his book, and ask yourself honestly: Is this a question *merely* of specifically English problems? Or is it not rather a question of typically Catholic concerns which, since the Council, have indeed become very much more perceptible, palpable, public, but are nevertheless very old? Were they not still specially emphasized precisely by Vatican I and by the Church of the Counter-Reformation as it was reaching its end? And are we not having to pay for this subsequently, now that Vatican II has taken over all too naturally some of these questions as solved by Vatican I? Can it be that the enormous excitement roused by Davis is understandable only because he has suddenly formulated questions closely affecting all too many in the Church, even if they have not ventured to express them—indeed, often have not even honestly thought them out?

Having spoken of the responsibility of the woman and the bishop, ought we not to look at the responsibility of Catholic theologians in general, who—Davis thought—had callously left him in the lurch, because they were unable to give him any adequate answers to his questions; indeed frequently they did not even venture to raise the truly urgent questions, to discuss them openly; as a result of cowardice and fear of censure, of ignorance and lack of exegetical and historical learning or simply of "ecclesial" naivety?

If we judge Davis' departure from the Church and its motives in complete truthfulness, if we do not push the responsibility onto his wife or onto Catholicism in England, if we do not close our eyes to reality by casting them down in prayer, if we venture with a strong, humble faith to face reality as it is, we cannot but draw the conclusion: it is a question here of a *challenge to the Catholic Church.* A challenge to the Church and her faith, proclaimed, practised, not by a poorly oriented outsider, but by a member of the Catholic Church herself, knowing her from within; not by a stranger, but by a leading man in the theological vanguard recognized by all trends in the Church; not from an extreme theological revolutionary, but from a notably modest and likable, reserved and yet courageous, man of the center, eager and ready for battle, who wants to remain loyal to himself and his vocation in uncompromising truthfulness.

The last sentence is written by one who became Charles Davis' friend and who is not prepared to withdraw that friendship, still less to disown him, because of his action, which I can understand only too well. We had and have corresponding questions, suffered and suffer under similar anxieties, frequently sought and seek similar theological solutions. We continue to pray graciously to be delivered from evil in the Church and hope for the renewal of Christendom in the spirit of the gospel of Jesus Christ. All this with one difference: Charles Davis is now looking for the Church of Jesus Christ *outside* the concrete (or, as he calls it, "institutional") Church.

In some respects of course it may be easier for a number of Catholic theologians resolutely to adhere to the Church than it was for Davis. They have found—and this touches on the first point we analyzed—among their closest friends men and women by whom they can be sure of being supported and upheld, by whom their remaining and working in the Church is continually made possible and fruitful. They have—and this concerns the second point—constantly found among the bishops those who at least do not disavow them; who, if necessary, protect them against attacks from above and below; who at least do not stand in the way of their work—perhaps even esteem, understand, use, promote it. They have—and this concerns the third point—mostly lived in countries where the concrete Catholic Church precisely in the last five years (in spite of all the opposition that still persists, from persons and institutions) has on the whole made more astonishing progress towards a new life in greater freedom, truth and humanity than has been known for a long time, perhaps for the past five hundred years.

In this sense, many theologians, very critical in regard to their Church, will readily admit—in spite of all their existential appreciation of the urgency and seriousness of Charles Davis' reasons (and they are primarily reasons of faith)—that they have never been seriously tempted to leave her: perhaps precisely not *although*, but *because,* as a result of their extensive exegetical and historical

studies, they have fewer illusions about the basis of the contemporary Church and her faith. That is why, at an early date, they had
put forward both practical and theological demands for reform
which were much more radical than those of Davis at that time, but
which they—not, of course, without radical *metanoia* even in regard to the teaching of the Church—considered as absolutely real-
izable within the concrete Church. I am by no means alone in
finding it more enjoyable now to be a Catholic theologian than I
did even a few years ago.

Our gigantic difficulties within the concrete Church and her
faith are not to be denied: all that Davis says of the pretentiousness
and the deficiencies of the institutional Church and of the papacy,
of the lack of truthfulness in the Church and the want of concern
for human beings, and particularly of the Vatican dogmas, are questions of the greatest importance. But it is here that I see precisely
the decisive point, and I know that in this respect I am in agreement with my revered Protestant friend, Karl Barth, when he spoke
to me about the desperate state of evangelical theology and the
Evangelical Church before the First World War: "At that time it
was enough to make one become a Catholic. And some of us did so
and got off the ship. I didn't."

Particularly in the storm, particularly in the towering difficulties
and a hopeless situation, the tossing and rolling ship—it is a question of human beings—needs us to *remain* in all truthfulness, to
share in steering it. Believing and trusting, to try *in the ship* to secure what has worked loose, to stop up leaks, to bring the ship back
to the right course laid down by its Lord, to make it seaworthy again.
Should not this be possible? What divides us is believing hope. Or
perhaps not? Charles Davis has got out of the ship, so rickety, all
too slow and unmaneuverable, not really to abandon it, but—this
is my conviction—better to aid it, while being outside and yet
linked with it. Now as before, he wants to be there for the human
beings who form the Church, to be associated with the people of
God.

It is a dangerous leap—particularly for theologians, who are not always the best swimmers—and many a one has finally been left behind in this test and in the end has been able to help neither himself nor his Church. But it may be that this is Charles Davis' vocation. There are often singular charisms, vocations to very extraordinary witness, prophetic commissions for which no one envies the person concerned, which scarcely anyone wholly understands. Charles Davis—so he expressly insists—has taken the decision solely for himself: he does not want any imitators and does not want to initiate a movement. He wanted only to follow his own conscience in complete truthfulness, to remain true to himself absolutely honestly, consistently and thoroughly, in order precisely in this way to be able to serve Christ and God and his fellow-men.

If we remain in the concrete Church, however, it is not merely out of loyalty; loyalty cannot be made a substitute for faith. *Credo ecclesiam:* because I believe *in* God, I believe *the* Church, her concrete existence and persistence through the Holy Spirit of God in spite of all the failures and errors of men and of their institution. And we, we who remain in this Church, certainly have our good reasons for doing so. They are not to be sought in our want of intelligence, of moral integrity, or of power to make an honest decision. It would require a book to expound these reasons and to answer the concrete questions raised by Davis. But perhaps it may be noted that, without knowing of Davis' decision, I wrote such a book; and just because it was not planned as an apologia, it may perform this service better.[4]

But who would be able or have the right to judge the man who has left us? In sympathy for a tormented human being, we have to respect his conscientious decision (a "question of conscience"), even though it is not ours. And at the same time we must not forget one thing: we, we who *in* the concrete Church believe *the* Church of Jesus Christ, ought to recognize the challenge that lies in this decision *against* the concrete Church. More than that. We ought to face this challenge to the concrete Church and her faith, not with evasive distinctions, but with a true, a truthful answer. And such a truthful answer cannot be given only with words, but in the last

resort only with deeds. What matters here too is not only to interpret the reality of the Church, but to alter it—in the light of the
gospel of Jesus Christ for the present time.

ADDITIONAL DOCUMENTATION

Charles Davis does not want his leaving the Church to be understood as a direct protest against priestly celibacy. Nevertheless, he
is aware that this step is in fact tantamount to an indirect and implicit protest against celibacy as a *universally binding law* (instead
of a freely accepted personal vocation, a charism). In the book
which he published in the meantime his basic arguments on voluntary celibacy (which he accepts) and legal (which he rejects) (pp.
30–32) agree in principle with the position which I had earlier felt
bound to make known to the press, in connection with the appearance of the encyclical of Pope Paul VI on celibacy. This communication is reproduced here in order to clarify the question, which is
likewise one of ecclesial truthfulness.

The merit of this encyclical lies in the fact that it gives expression
openly to the difficulties in regard to celibacy. It does not, however,
solve the problems, but renders them more acute by the very fact
of stating them. The gospel allows for a personal vocation of the
individual to celibacy in the service of men, as Jesus and Paul lived
it, providing an example also for the present time. But both Jesus and
Paul expressly assure complete freedom to each individual. A universal *law* of celibacy contradicts this expressly assured freedom—
celibacy as a free *charism*. Peter and the apostles were and remained
married, even when their imitation of Christ was perfect, and this
remained for many centuries the pattern for the leader of the congregation. But what primarily had its freely chosen place first in the
monastic communities was extended in later centuries as an express
prohibition of marriage to the whole of the clergy and partly forced
upon them. In our conciliar and post-conciliar age, however, the
opinion is coming to prevail more and more, even within the Catholic
Church, among clergy and laity, that this extraordinarily radical, legal
intrusion into the rights of human personality infringes not only the

original liberal order of the Church but also the modern conception of the freedom of the individual.

In the present state of the Church three problems above all are raised by the present canonical ruling, and they ought to be solved:

1. The Church in recent years has lost an alarmingly increasing number of very often highly qualified candidates for the priesthood, whom today she needs more than ever.

2. The number of office-holders who subsequently give up office in the Church or are landed in inescapable difficulties runs into tens of thousands (4,000 requests from priests simply for legitimate marriage now lie before the Roman Curia; in Italy alone, however, the number of priests who have left without dispensation is estimated today at 6,000-15,000—statistics have never been published).

3. In view partly of the enormous shortage of priests and of the notably large proportion of elderly clergy the question of married or non-married priests must give way to the *primary* obligation of the Church to provide leaders at all to the congregations.

Other arguments might be discussed. On this point anyway there will be no rest in the Catholic Church until celibacy is again left to the free choice of the individual and the canon law in this respect— introduced in very problematic circumstances—reversed.

For the further procedure the *collegial* treatment of the problem is suggested, in the synod of bishops meeting in autumn in Rome: as is known, discussion was prevented at the council. Collegiality in the Church requires too that the priests themselves—who are involved— be questioned in a secret ballot, whether they desire a *law* of celibacy or want to leave celibacy to the *decision of the individual*.[5]

In connection with the position here adopted, 1 have frequently been asked by what right one contradicts a papal encyclical. The reasons may be briefly indicated here:

1. According to universal Catholic teaching a papal encyclical is not an infallible ecclesiastical document, but in principle fallible.

2. According to universal Catholic teaching, the law of celibacy is not a divine, but a purely ecclesiastical law, which can again be abolished at any time.

3. a. The discussion on celibacy desired by many bishops was for-bidden at the Council by the same Pope who many times invokes the Council to support his view in the encyclical.

b. The papal encyclical came out immediately before the assembly of the synod of bishops, at which discussion of the law of celibacy again remained excluded from the agenda and in fact was again not permitted, although since the encyclical opposition to the law of celibacy in many countries has increased rather than slackened.

c. Hence for many bishops and theologians, but also for the whole Catholic Church, the question emerges as to whether the collegiality of the supreme government of the Church, decided on at the Second Vatican Council, is to remain—particularly in questions which are of the greatest importance in the Church—a phrase that has no practical meaning. Frankly stated: Is the Church now as before to accept "lone decisions," made in the style of the *ancien régime,* simply in silence or grumblingly, depressed or hoping for better times; *or* ought the objections both to the authoritative but fallible view presented and to the mode of procedure to be brought forward, tactfully but publicly— experience shows that this is the only way to make an impression in Rome—*in aedificationem ecclesiae,* for the building up of the Church?

We know that the Pope, who is inspired with the best intentions, has the priests' needs very much at heart, and hence we think that a Church government not concerned with prestige but with the matter itself, not with its system but with human beings, ought to be interested in the second alternative. And I am glad to say that up to now the attitude I have adopted has not led to a *monitum* either from Rome or from a bishop (but of course, because a taboo has been infringed, from some notoriously fanatical Catholics—especially women without families and some older clerics).

4. I would have been only too glad to remain silent on this as on other occasions. One reflects anyway, alone and with others, before publicly intervening in any debate; and only the cause or—better— the human beings involved, make it possible to overcome the resistance that one always feels to a public engagement in heated questions and its not necessarily pleasant consequences. It is not a fanatical sense of mission that ought to move a theologian at such moments, only the sober, unpretentious, realistic-pragmatic theological sense of duty.

5. Perhaps a brief personal plea may be added, to the many people who privately and with their friends complain of one thing and another. It is important to write encouraging letters to those who take a public stand (a very thick dossier has emerged on the abolition of the law of celibacy). It would be still more to the point to take a

stand with more or less publicity, in a letter to a paper or to the bishops, or in some other way—but in any event publicly. We shall get any further only if as many as possible are publicly committed.[6]

NOTES

1. Charles Davis, *A Question of Conscience* (New York, Harper, 1968).
2. Cf. the additional documentation at the end of this chapter.
3. Even in his new book Davis does not examine this positive hypothesis.
4. H. Küng, *Die Kirche* (Herder, Freiburg-Basle-Vienna, 1967); *The Church*, trans. Ray and Rosaleen Ockenden (New York, Sheed and Ward, 1968).
5. "The *Spiegel* has ascertained from the Emnid Institute at Bielefeld what Germans—especially German Catholics—are thinking about priests and marriage. Although otherwise in answer to such inquiries many Germans do not express any opinion, on the question of celibacy only 1% refused to give an answer. Total result: 84% of Germans think that priests ought to be allowed to marry; nine months ago another inquiry indicated only 73%. More surprising than the fact that 95% of Protestants and 96% of those without denomination were for the abolition of celibacy is that more than two-thirds (69%) of German Catholics were in favor of priests marrying. At the same time there is (contrary to the widespread pre-judgment of the clergy) no difference of opinion between unmarried Catholics (70% in favor) and married Catholics (71%), between men (71%) and women (68%). . . . The trend is clear. The younger Catholics are, so much the more strongly do they approve the marriage of priests. The majority, which with the 60's and 70's is only 59%, rises to 69% with the 50's to 59's, to 70% with the 35's to 49's, to 73% with the 25's to 34's, and to 77% with the 18's to 24's.

"There are very different attitudes with different callings. Most frequently the marriage of priests is approved by skilled workers and technicians (80%); the lowest percentage is found among agricultural workers (52%). Correspondingly, in places where there are less than 2,000 inhabitants there are relatively fewer opponents of celibacy (60%) than in the towns and cities with 20,000 to 500,000 inhabitants (77%) and in the large cities (68%).

"But whatever Catholic group is questioned, there is constantly a clear majority for the abolition of compulsory celibacy. Even Catholics who regularly go to church are more than fifty per cent (58%) in favor of priests marrying." *Der Spiegel* N[r] 46, 1967.

The latest figures of priests giving up their office are alarming. In Holland in 1966 there were 60 all told. In 1967 there were already 145; many of these have in the meantime married. In the United States during these years there were at least 711, of whom 322 have already married. The figure in 1967 was more than double that of the previous year. Exact statistics have not yet been published for the other countries in which the same problems exist.

The problem of theology students preparing for the Church's ministry is no less disturbing. Since an extraordinarily strong opposition to celibacy is everywhere observable, incalculable difficulties (and in particular a serious decline in vocations) must be expected unless the law is quickly and resolutely abolished.

A simple example to illustrate the situation: in an opinion poll of the faculty of Catholic theology in the University of Tübingen 172 out of 180 candidates for the priesthood were against the law of celibacy; 327 members of the faculty—that is, about 65%—took part in the inquiry. The vote for a free decision of conscience was 297, women members of the faculty being unanimously in favor. Votes for a "free decision" were given by 38 theology students, 73 male lay theologians, 14 priests and 172 candidates for the priesthood. Only 4 lay theologians, 3 priests and 8 candidates for the priesthood voted in favor of the Church's laws.

6. Cf. H. Küng, *Theologe und Kirche* (Theologische Meditationen 3, Einsiedeln, 1964).

II/Transvaluation of the Virtues

THERE ARE some virtues which have greater prospects than others. Among these is truthfulness. Discovered in its real sense at a comparatively late stage, it is one of the basic virtues of modern man. Only when there is a future for truthfulness in the Church will there be a genuine Church of the future.

It is a fallacy to suppose that every virtue is equally important at all times and that the Church is saddled with an unchangeable, static framework of virtues. Even morality is historically determined through and through. The word "virtue" itself has frequently changed its meaning: beginning with pagan antiquity and continuing, by way of the patristic and medieval syntheses of the ancient ideas of virtue with the Christian ethos, up to modern times, when the term has lost much of its credit—despite the efforts on the part of M. Sailer, F. Schleiermacher, M. Scheler and N. Hartmann towards its revaluation.

At the same time, the word originally had nothing at all of the derisory, almost absurd meaning of the modern "virtuousness" ("a virtuous maiden"); it had none of the flavor of "well-behaved," "worthy," "delicate," "timid," "cautious," "passive." As the German word *Tugend* comes from *taugen* ("to be capable") and originally meant quite generally any ability (*Tauglichkeit*) and proficiency (*Tüchtigkeit*), so the corresponding Greek word *arete* means the ability and proficiency (mental or corporal), not only of man but also of animals and tools: a capacity which is then restricted by Socrates to man's moral proficiency; the corresponding Latin *virtus* even means expressly "manliness" (cf. the *virtù* of Renaissance man, bursting with vigor, from which again the concept of virtuosity is derived). If the word "virtue" cannot be avoided and if today it is used generally for the constant, but ever freshly to be realized, basic moral attitudes of man, then it must be understood precisely in the light of its origin, in its strong, positive and active sense.

Again, however, the systems of virtue underwent fundamental changes. We need only compare the diversity of approaches.

Socrates revalues the aristocratic class virtues and turns them into civic moral virtues, recognized by the *polis*. Plato, in the light of his trichotomous theory of the soul which is reflected in his political theory, brings in the four virtues which, since the time of St. Ambrose, have been known as the cardinal (pivotal) virtues: temperance (for the instinctive-appetitive stratum of the soul or the laboring class), fortitude (for the spirited stratum of the soul or the warrior class), wisdom (for the rational stratum of the soul or the teaching class), and justice as regulating all the rest. Aristotle establishes empirically an open system of more than a dozen ethical and dianoetical (intellectual) virtues, in which each virtue provides the mean between two extremes, between too much and too little. Stoicism reduces all virtues to a single one (*apatheia*—absence of passion). The Neoplatonism of Plotinus or Porphyry works out an ascending scheme of civic, purifying, contemplative and exemplary virtues.

After Augustine, Gregory, Peter Lombard and Radulfus Ardens, Aquinas unites Platonic, Aristotelian, Stoic and Neoplatonic elements into a closed system of natural and supernatural, theological (faith, hope and charity) and moral virtues (according to the scheme of the four cardinal virtues).

Finally, there are the modern variations of the traditional four by Geulincx in the seventeenth century (diligence, obedience, justice, humility) and Schleiermacher in the nineteenth (wisdom, love, circumspection, courage).

Historical reflection makes it clear that systems of virtue in the course of time have always been constructed from a quite definite, limited standpoint, which again was dependent on a time-conditioned anthropology, at the expense of virtues which had no place at all in the scheme concerned or existed only at the periphery: hence truthfulness does not play a constitutive role in any of the systems mentioned. Obviously there are connections and diversities of rank among the individual virtues, there are groups of virtues arranged from different standpoints. But an overlapping, closed system of virtues does not do justice to the complexity and variation of the human reality. Like Aristotle in his day, Nicolai Hartmann and Otto Friedrich Bollnow in their modern theories of virtue are not trying to establish a closed system, but to frame a phenomenological description based on particular groups.

Yet the *individual virtues,* too, are themselves not timeless realities, but are exposed to the changes of moral consciousness. Unremittingly, in accordance with the varying situations, they must be conceptually determined and practically realized. No virtue can be pinned down in history. Codified morality and conventional virtues can become questionable, as Christian theologians ought to have observed before Nietzsche (who does not simply reject virtue). In a new age many designations of the virtues are again differently understood and therefore also differently evaluated. The individual virtues in the course of history have their ups and downs, they change their appearance constantly in the understanding of men and thus exhibit the whole wealth of possibilities open to man's choice.

Moreover, virtues come and go, but this does not necessarily involve either a strengthening or a decline of morals. Ancient, venerable virtues fade: words wear out and the significance of virtues for human existence in a new age is no longer understood (e.g., humility, by and large, today); they have lost their formative power, they no longer play any role worth mentioning in the moral consciousness of a new generation, although we cannot claim that men have become worse on that account. But the converse is also true. New virtues turn up: they become visible in the light of new

needs of human life as it is transformed, and perhaps at first are not
recognized as virtues at all; they have borrowed names, and in
ethics they are not yet cited as virtues; and yet for the new generation they already form basic moral attitudes which have taken the
place of former virtues (so today, for example, fairness, objectivity,
frankness, propriety).

All this does not mean any arbitrary relativization, and still less
the abolition of the virtues. It is much more a question of a core of
basic human attitudes which have to be freshly realized in constantly changing historical situations and thence take on a new
shape historically determined in the light of man's understanding
at the time. If on the one hand we have to devote our special attention to the virtues which threaten to disappear from the consciousness of a generation and which—in given circumstances—cannot
be replaced by others, then on the other hand we must also look to
the virtues which in a new age imply a new human possibility.[1]

Truthfulness is a recent, a present-day virtue. If we are to take
the concepts in a quite strict sense (which generally does not
happen in ordinary use),[2] then truthfulness is more than honesty
and straightforwardness. Honesty and straightforwardness concern
man's outward behavior in regard to the other person, straightforwardness emphasizing more than honesty the disposition behind
this behavior. Truthfulness, however, concerns first and last the
attitude of man *to himself*: it is the way in which a person is placed
in regard to himself. A person is truthful, therefore, not simply outwardly—in relation to his fellow-men—but inwardly—in relation
to himself. Yet this does not simply mean a natural openness or a
natural harmony with oneself; in that case we speak not so much of
a person's truthfulness as of his frankness or genuineness, both of
which can be completely unconscious. Truthfulness, however, consciously seeks frankness and genuineness, against all opposition:
hence truthfulness is the transparency of a human being (or also of
a human community), maintained for himself and thus also for
others against opposition.

During the Second Vatican Council I asked my friend, the original drafter of the conciliar Declaration on Religious Liberty, the

American theologian John Courtney Murray (who died too soon), what was to be thought of a certain American archbishop. He answered, with a smile: "He is an absolutely honest man. He would never lie except for the good of the Church." This remark, as shrewd as it is ironical, envisages the very opposite of truthfulness. The opposite of truthfulness is not simply lying but untruthfulness. Here we must make some even more precise distinctions. When do we talk of untruth, of untruthfulness, of lying?

If we are to differentiate between these concepts, we must first distinguish truth from truthfulness. We speak of truth (in the traditional conception, which is adequate here), if a statement ("objectively") agrees with its object. If this is not the case, then we speak of untruth in the sense of incorrectness and of ("objective") falsity. On the other hand, we speak of truthfulness if a statement ("subjectively") agrees with the opinion of the speaker. If this is not the case, we speak of untruthfulness in the sense of mendacity, dissimulation or hypocrisy. A lie, then, like the truth in the above conception, concerns the particular statement; at the same time a lie— the intent of which is to deceive for the sake of some advantage —aims outwardly, at another person. A lie is an untrue statement to deceive another for the sake of my advantage or his disadvantage. Untruthfulness is quite different: it envisages not the particular statement, but the human being as a person, as a whole in his basic attitude, and at the same time it aims not outwardly, but inwardly, at the relation of a man towards himself.

There is, then, a difference between lying and untruthfulness. To come back to the example just cited: a poor wretch—and any of us may be such now and again in ordinary life—can lie because he wants to get out of something or to gain some advantage; he can even do this frequently, can even be an inveterate liar, and yet he need not for that reason be really an *untruthful* person. Why? Because he knows that he is lying, because he admits it to himself, because he accepts responsibility for his lying, because it is—so to speak—an "honest" lie and he is an "honest" liar. And this is just what our ecclesiastic is not.

The latter is rather the example—we are not judging him, but using him merely as a very instructive model—of an untruthful person. He lies too, but he does not admit to himself that he is lying; he denies his lie to himself, he lies it away from himself; he has explained everything neatly, so that he can seem quite honest to himself. But he is not wholly successful. The semblance of honesty is too facile a deception and an unadmitted feeling of injustice persists. In any case such a man is no longer in complete harmony with himself: he is in a twilight zone in regard to himself, not wholly transparent to himself; he is inwardly untruthful, and many of his often very irrational reactions must be understood in the light of this fact. Such a man remains untruthful even when he is silent, indeed even when he tells the truth; for his untruthfulness does not in fact consist in particular, deceptive, false statements, but constitutes his discordant, personal basic attitude.

At the same time the specific feature of such an untruthful ecclesiastic—in this respect resembling exactly the untruthful statesman—is that he was driven to untruth, not for his own advantage (he is not a malicious, vicious person), but—so to speak—for the common good, which he has particularly to defend in the Church (or in the state). This good of the Church (or of the state), this *raison de l'Église*, is what makes him lie with confidence, without being disturbed in his conscience. Indeed he does not do it for his own sake but for the sake of the great whole for which he stands. He need not accept responsibility for it: the institution does that. Thus for the sake of the Church he manages to deny his lie to himself, to lie it away, to lie it into truth. And precisely for this reason his lie is not an honest lie and he is not an honest liar, but a profoundly untruthful person.

As long as in former times there was not the modern tension between individual consciousness and community, but harmony with society was self-evident, truthfulness could not yet acquire importance as a virtue. In this sense truthfulness is a modern virtue, possible only from that time onwards when a self-conscious subjectivity began to develop. But, precisely as a modern virtue, truthfulness more than the other virtues is of absolutely fundamental importance for the future and for the Church of the future.

We would not be taking truthfulness in the Church seriously enough if we were to understand it merely as one virtue among others or even simply as a particularly important virtue. Since truthfulness does not concern man's state in this world and his relation to it—as, for instance, do the civic virtues (order, thrift, cleanliness) or also diligence, courage, circumspection, equanimity, modesty, or even finally prudence and wisdom—but the relation of man to himself, it is absolutely fundamental for the ethos of men and of the human community. If the relation of man to himself and hence that of the community to itself is disturbed, if this relation to oneself is no longer clear and transparent, then the moral existence of man or of the community is threatened all along the line. Without this inner truthfulness, the civic virtues, and the other virtues too, are endangered at their roots: they are no longer possible in an authentic fashion.

Hence it is clear that the Church (like the state) is corrupted in her most essential reality when the spirit of untruthfulness enters into her. Not simply because there is more lying (which is also involved), but because the person and the community are softened, broken down in their innermost and basic morality and thus lose all moral restraint.

The spirit of untruthfulness—as in the totalitarian political systems, of which we have had quite enough experience in our century—can enter the Church also, through *authoritarianism.* Authority simply determines what is truth, and truth in authoritarianism is what suits authority: its organization, its regime, its system. What agrees with this authoritarian "truth of the system" is promoted, propagated by every means. What contradicts this "truth of the system" is brought to book, prohibited, persecuted, suppressed, concealed by every means. Thus untruthfulness is spread in a community and infects everything.

People adapt themselves. They avoid telling the truth, contradicting authority: this is dangerous, it is not true to the party-line, not according to "the mind of the Church." To act otherwise is to risk something, to become unpopular with those "at the top"—and not only there. It is preferable to remain silent, even though silence is ambiguous—or indeed unambiguous, implicit consent. People get out of the way of any sort of conflict, avoid all swimming against the stream, indeed—since it is difficult to avoid if the opportune moment for dissociation has not been seized—people even co-operate in one way or another: here or there they compound untruthfulness, inwardly by telling themselves and others that nothing can be done to prevent it; and anyway it is not all that bad—in the last resort there is even something good about it, greater disaster can in fact be prevented and in the end all will turn out well—and so on. So finally we justify to ourselves the untruthfulness of the system and our own untruthfulness, by no means simply out of malice, but rather because of weakness, compliance, desire for peace, tractability, obedience. Is there anyone who has never felt these temptations in himself?

The authoritarian system, however, is not necessary to bring untruthfulness to the surface in a community. *Opportunism* in its most general form is sufficient. Adaptation to an authoritarian or totalitarian system is not necessary. An uncritical, irresponsible adaptation to an environment, to a trend, to a social, political, cultural, scientific tendency of the time, to the spirit of the age, to a particular combination of power: this in itself suffices to lead people into untruthfulness, into being no longer quite honest with themselves, no longer wholly transparent to themselves. Thus opportunism and authoritarianism are closely related. The opportunism of the many makes possible the authoritarianism of the few and the authoritarianism of the few promotes the opportunism of the many. Authoritarianism and opportunism can even occur in the one person and—even in the office-holder—wonderfully complement one another. It is then a question of being authoritarian towards those below and opportunist towards those above; that is what is commonly described as the posture of the ecclesiastical cyclist, bending over above and pedalling below.

Untruthfulness means—in the human community, in the Church —not only irresponsibility but a softening, a destruction, a loss of identity, of selfhood, of inner substance: corruption of good nature through un-nature. Only in truthfulness does a human community, does the Church, come to itself, constantly renew its identity. Only in truthfulness, piercing the darkness of un-nature, does the luminous nature of the Church reveal itself. The greatness of the task is plain.

NOTES

1. Throughout this section the excellent book by O. F. Bollnow, *Wesen und Wandel der Tugenden* (Frankfurt on the Main, 1962), pp. 9-30, has proved particularly inspiring.
2. Cf. O. F. Bollnow, *op. cit.*, pp. 135-154.

III/Truthfulness as Peril

TRUTHFULNESS can bring to light the Church's good nature only if it does not degenerate into fanaticism for truthfulness, which insofar as it too is abroad in the Church must be counted as part of her dark un-nature. As we see it, untruthfulness is a special danger for Catholic theology and the Catholic Church, fanaticism for truthfulness a special danger in Protestant theology and the Protestant Churches. Obviously, in neither case does this statement hold true without exceptions: there is much untruthfulness among Protestants also and not a little fanaticism for truthfulness among Catholics, but on the whole the emphasis is different.

Since we have already had to criticize so much, and shall have to criticize still more, in Catholic theology and in the Catholic Church this seems a good time—so that it cannot be misunderstood on the Protestant side—to attempt to restore the balance. Otherwise the result would be (as is frequent especially with a type of Protestant triumphalism) that people would note with satisfaction that the Catholics are now (at last) becoming concerned about what has for so long been of concern to Protestants—and so the Protestant Reformation is confirmed once again, and that is the end of the matter. But the Reformation goes on! So Schleiermacher in his time demanded—though it need not necessarily continue in his sense. In any case, factually and practically, the Protestant Churches and Protestant theology have only too often replaced the *ecclesia semper reformanda*—which should be understood as a constant imperative—with the satisfied, self-assured, immobile indicative, *ecclesia reformata (est),* thus serving neither the cause of the Reformation nor that of Christendom.

In other words, we see far too little activity in the Protestant Churches, in which today—at least in Europe—the ecumenical impetus is notably slighter than in the Catholic Church, and in which people are governed by fear of the more dynamic Church. The new effort in the Catholic Church and in her theology involves a demand, a very urgent desideratum and postulate, put to the Protestant Churches and Protestant theology not to remain passive on their side, but to begin to give more serious attention to their own specific need and function in the light of the gospel, to exert greater efforts, in a wholly concrete way, towards *truth* in the Church and *the truth of the Church.*

In fact, if there is anything which is a disavowal of the Protestant Reformation and which is discrediting the Protestant Churches also today, it is their dividedness in the matter of truth, the plainly chaotic situation in proclamation and teaching, the "doctrinal chaos"—as it is called by Protestants themselves—in the Protestant Churches. These incredible contradictions in all the different pulpits and theological faculties, all the contrasts in faith of the different Churches and congregations which emerge from this, all the constantly new formations of parties and schools, and all the sectarianism in theology and practice: no theologian should venture to justify theologically this contradiction and division in truth (possibly not even from the New Testament).

Certainly, in the light particularly of the New Testament, we do not need a uniform Church, still less a uniform theology: doctrinal and practical diversity, tensions too, contrasts too, are possible and in a sense necessary. But what kind of Church is it in which the one believes what another regards as superstition, heresy or even unbelief, and vice-versa? As soon as it is a question of division on the truth of faith itself, which leads the different Churches, congregations, groups, to cease to maintain communion, eucharistic communion, ecclesial communion (like the contrasting congregations of

Jerusalem and the Diaspora, like Jewish Christians and Gentile Christians, as Peter and Paul maintained it), then there can be no more talk of justification, but only of confessing guilt and doing penance. There can be no appeal to the New Testament in order to justify division in the truth of faith. Despite all its contrasts the New Testament testifies to a basic unity of the Church and her faith. Division arises not from the New Testament itself but as the result of a quite definite selection, *haeresis,* of certain elements opposed in the balanced unity of Scripture, which are turned into absolutes. However, monotonous uniformity and egalitarianism in "Catholic" truth cannot be corrected by Protestant selectivity and dividedness but only through the realization of a unity in tension-charged multiplicity and diversity. In the truth of faith, then, Protestant concentration is combined with Catholic breadth.

But this unity in tension-charged multiplicity and diversity can be realized only in a truthfulness that does not degenerate into fanaticism for truthfulness at the expense of ecclesial communion. Only the theology whose truthfulness is positively involved in the ecclesial community, which does not merely cherish its esoteric scholarship in critical scepticism, resignation or aggressiveness at the periphery of the Church, will master this heavy task. The professional theologian, too, in the last resort, has received Christian truth, not through spiritual enlightenment or his own personal invention, but through the proclamation and tradition of the believing community. He is and remains bound to this. And this on the whole is what he really wants to be in the Protestant Church as well.

Yet serving the ecclesial community by a simple, honest striving in truthfulness is not sufficient to get onto the track of truth. Certainly a theology really serves the Church only if it is a seriously critical theology, seriously allowing for the failure of the Church of men also in the discovery of truth and maintenance of truth and distinguishing in the light of the original Christian message the true faith of the Church from all superstition, heresy and unbelief, by decisively applying all the aids of exegetical, historical, systematic and practical criticism. But this criticism will attain this goal in the

Church only when the theologian himself is positively committed and remains in the Church, when in the concrete he is also inwardly united with and indebted to the ecclesial community, by striving not least for the unity of this Church of his in the truth of faith. What this means in the concrete may be briefly explained.

Only the theologian who approaches the Church's Scriptures selected in the Old and New Testament Canon as a basically sound testimony to the original Christian truth—he alone—has then also the right and duty within this Church to inquire in complete truthfulness, with all the aids of scientific criticism, how far these Scriptures of the Old and New Testament attest God's word more directly and clearly, or more indirectly and obscurely, in its original or derived form; how far human weakness and frailty on the part of the authors, diversity of character, of environment, of theological conception, of communal faith, of different traditions and so on determine the writing. If a theologian *a priori* despises or disregards the discernment of spirits and selection of Scriptures, which the early Church carried out in an extremely wearisome and complex testing of its canon and which the Church of all later centuries has constantly ratified afresh, with advantage to herself, his truthfulness in theological investigation will be able to aid the Church and her truth only to a very limited extent.

Only the theologian who takes account seriously and positively of the professions of faith of the primitive Church and of their lines of demarcation against heresy and makes use of these in order to follow the difficult path between truth and the various forms of untruth—he alone—has also then the right and duty, within the Church, to determine critically in all truthfulness how far these professions, confessions, and definitions attest the original Christian truth, exactly or inexactly, appropriately or inappropriately; how far they confess or conflict, affirm or react, render explicit or polemize; how far the human weaknesses and frailties of the Church at the time here too have demanded their tribute; how far a particular contemporary situation, the raising of a question, tradition, was a determining factor and so on. If a theologian despises or disregards the boundary posts and danger signals which the Church of former times set up, often in the midst of the greatest distress, concerned and struggling for the truth of faith, in order to distinguish good from bad interpretation, he need not be surprised if, in spite of all his personal truthfulness, he nevertheless ultimately contributes more to confusing the truth in the Church than to finding it.

Only the theologian who seriously, positively and to the best of his ability masters the theology of former times and is thereby spared beginning at zero, without experience in a short life, from a narrow, subjective perspective, who in this way avoids being sidetracked into areas already well trodden and fully explored, since he concerns himself with the important findings of former times— he alone within the Church has also the right and duty to inquire critically into the extent to which the great theologians of former times are witnesses of the original Christian truth, clearly or obscurely, unambiguously or ambiguously, intelligibly or less intelligibly, emphatically or hesitantly, powerfully or weakly; the extent to which, on them too, human weakness and the frailties to which all men are subject have exerted a dubious influence; the extent to which they have been determined—fertilized but limited too—by their tradition, their milieu, their experience, their psyches, thought-structures, *Weltanschauung*. If a theologian despises or disregards the positive and negative experiences and conclusions of his fathers and brothers in theology, particularly the experiences and conclusions of theology in the Christian sister-Churches, his truthfulness will rightly represent in the Church never more than a very dubious, sometimes odd, but rarely credible authority.

How important it is, however, for truthfulness not to degenerate into fanaticism for truthfulness—and this has so many forms and possibilities—but to prove its true nature in the community. Otherwise the consequences set in irrecusably which bring the credibility of a theology and Church into serious doubt. Some only of these consequences will be noted, brought out in bolder outlines under a series of headings: these would certainly hold more for Europe than for America, more for lesser than for greater theologians. At the same time, it may readily be admitted that the phenomena to be designated naturally have other roots than *merely* excessive truthfulness.

Intellectual naivety. In spite of theoretical statements to the contrary, people in practice are convinced that they "possess" truth, that they are far in advance of the theology of the other Church, that they do not need seriously to study the other literature, that the others really only need to follow. People do not notice how they are dazzled only by their own—admittedly important —conclusions and therefore overlook, do not take seriously, do not work up, important or even more important questions, concerns, demands of others; they do not see how in this way, in spite of their good intentions, their own truth is somewhere diluted through reduction, concentration, undialectical presentation, through mental inhibition, narrow-mindedness, through a singular theological color-blindness. But is it not precisely ignorance which leads most easily to intellectual pride?

Theological isolation. A person is thrown back on himself, isolated in the Church, in spite of having some friends who are interested in theology. But importance is attached to originality; marking oneself off from others is more important, more scientific, than working out what binds people together. Theology is considered, not as a common task, as a great piece of teamwork across the frontiers of nations and Churches, but as a battlefield on which in the last resort everyone fights against everyone else with ever new weapons and methods, behind ever new fronts and groupings. Where the Church is less important, the theological school becomes all the more important: here one lives, fights for its dogmas; the other school is a worse opponent than the other Church. Thus one becomes deaf to other questions, terminologies, arguments, conclusions. But no one is as certain of his solutions as the person who is deaf to problems.

Weakening of the Church. Instead of the Church being critically and constructively helped by theology, she is thrown into confu-

sion: theologians develop into minor popes, the Church becomes a
Church of professors, faith mainly a matter for discussion. And infallibility is appropriated not by one but by several persons. While
some fear an untruthful obscurantism, others fear an untrue "other
gospel." Instead of listening to one another, talking across one another; instead of learning from one another, teaching against one
another; instead of co-operation, dispersal; instead of active commitment in the Church, endless discussion. So the Church on the
one hand becomes the affair of small incapsulated groups of pietists
and on the other mainly of interested intellectuals; and then only
too often faith stands opposed to faith, pulpit to pulpit, faculty to
faculty, in hopeless divisions and in a dispute that no one can ar-
bitrate. All at the expense of human beings, to whom such a Church
then also has not much more to say and with which they come into
contact at best on family feasts, or on Good Friday or Remem-
brance Sunday. Against this disintegration of the Church community we can take comfort with theories about the "cell" and with
biblical study in a small circle.

In short then: because of her failure in truth, anything but a
truthful Church. All this is of course a caricature—fortunately, a
gross exaggeration of the reality found in any Protestant Church.
But the picture conveys a serious warning; it is composed of individual features which are all drawn from reality. And this is meant
to emphasize the fact that truthfulness alone is not sufficient. Truthfulness too can be ridden to death. Fanaticism for truthfulness occurs at the expense of truth, of human beings, of congregations, of
the Church, of Christendom. Fanaticism for truthfulness arises
often—in virtue of the best intentions—in opposition to a hard-
frozen orthodoxy to which truth is all-important and truthfulness
less so. Yet precisely fanaticism for truthfulness, to which truthfulness is all-important and truth less so, leads for its own part
through its false shock-effect to a new freezing up of orthodoxy,
since it is thought that only orthodox ecclesiasticism can redeem us
from such fanaticism for truth.

We are considering in this book the demand for greater truthfulness as a basic requirement addressed to Catholic theology and the Church. But it has now become more than clear that the reverse side of this demand is turned towards Protestantism and its theology. Since we cannot be turning constantly, throughout the book, to this reverse side (though that might, perhaps, have been desirable), it must be clearly, once and for all, brought into the field of vision. But lest it should seem as if the problems were not recognized within Protestantism, the testimonies of four Protestant authors are cited here at length: they draw attention to the same thing from different standpoints and in a very different light.

The Protestant Church historian Franz Lau brings out the fact that Martin Luther's new truthfulness in the Church of that time served to point a direction, but if it is exaggerated it can bring the Church into great distress. Karl Jaspers is able to show, perhaps even more clearly than the theologian, the extent to which the fanatical passion for truth is opposed to the pure quest for truth and is destructive in its influence. For Dietrich Bonhoeffer, who maintained his truthfulness as a theologian unto death, the decisive factor is to tell the truth in the community in the right way, so that a ruthless veracity does not destroy the living truth among human beings and betray the community. Karl Barth—who often enough has criticized the Church unsparingly—finally emphasizes how a critical theology in particular, which has to raise the question of truth in relation to the Church, must carry out its task in communion with the congregation, with the Church.

GRANDEUR AND PERIL OF LUTHER'S TRUTHFULNESS (ACCORDING TO F. LAU)

Luther's unique significance for Christianity lies first of all in his sharpening of a man's conscience in regard to truth. This is the true meaning of the well-known and currently somewhat controversial saying, that Luther's religion was "conscience religion." What does that mean? Luther taught the individual simply to let the truth prevail in all his believing, his convictions, his actions, his entire life. He charged the church with the same responsibility. It is the truth that we must confess; for it we are commanded to contend; for the truth's sake we must die if necessary, and for the truth's sake a church must be prepared to perish. What is Truth? Truth is the great objective reality of God.

For Luther, however, it pertains to the truth that it becomes certain to me. Luther was far from sending each individual on his own way and letting him without warning and counsel shut himself up within his own fantasies. He received the truth gratefully as a gift of grace that had been bestowed upon his church as a community. But unless we are personally grasped by the truth there is no truth for us. And if Luther had done no more than demonstrate in his own person the extreme case where one must stand alone for the truth, he would nevertheless have impressed this fact deeply upon the consciousness of all men who have experienced and understood his struggle, that truth as personal conviction becomes reality. And if truth is recognized, then only truth is valid—not expediency, not the possibility of becoming rich and happy by some other means than that of the confession of truth, not the ideal of an all-domineering and maternal church for whose unity one would be required under certain circumstances to sacrifice the truth or part of it, but the truth alone and obedience to it.

The acceptance of this principle brought the churches that related themselves to Luther into grave perils. The confessional antagonism within the evangelical world has its ultimate ground in the conscience concerning the truth, sharpened by Luther. Is there such a thing as an over-sharpened conscience concerning the truth, which can turn into orthodox bigotry? Is there a fanaticism for the truth that denies love? It would not be good a priori and without very exact testing to place a stamp of approval upon all of Luther's decisions, for example, in the controversy with the Swiss. That Luther on account of his sensitive conscience for the truth could become very harsh against all his opponents, and did become so harsh in the last analysis for that reason only, obliges us to take his harshness with utter seriousness, but cannot mean that he was infallible in his concrete decisions, let alone that all such decisions should be accepted uncritically in the future history of Luther's church! What is actually binding and obligatory is Luther's categorical conscience in regard to the truth.[1]

THE DESTRUCTIVENESS OF FANATICISM FOR
TRUTH (ACCORDING TO KARL JASPERS)

Fanatical passion for truth has the character of indictment, rejection, annihilation, of rendering contemptible and derision, of moral pretension, of ostentatious superiority; this passion satisfies the instinct for self-assertion and belittling the other person. This polemical aspect of truth-fanaticism gives it a negating character. It is a mark of this truth to be immediately partisan. It asks more about the opponent than about the truth. The possession of this truth provides a platform in that it is raised up above the mass of what is untrue. The form in which such truth is communicated is from the conqueror's position.

Opposed to this is the serenity of the real vision of truth, the purity of the quest for truth that is linked with reality. This rest and unrest does not possess the truth, but acquires it through continuing the quest. It lives on a positive factor that develops. Negation and polemics are pure consequences.

Characteristic of fanaticism for truth is affectivity, which permits no one else to speak any longer, will not listen, but only wants to be heard: it sticks to affirmation, in all discussion remains in fact outside discussion. It is a polemic without communication.

On the other hand, the quest for truth that is linked with reality wants boundless communication with the other person, wants to hear, wants to question acquired positions and to bring all fixedness to the point at which it has to be sacrificed.

If truth means a firm stand, then in the fanatical passion for truth that firm stand is a forced, blind standing until the moment comes for a fall. In the genuine quest for truth a firm stand means an open gaze until the moment comes for questioning and transforming movement. Firmly standing fanaticism comes to a fall, without contributing anything to the transmission of what is true. The firmly standing quest for truth may through dying become a link in the chain of the transmission of truth.

The fanatical passion for truth, in its action, seizes on all forms of the quest for truth, by distorting, bartering, isolating them, making them absolutes. It can even adopt the mask of a quest for truth, if the possession of truth has shrunk to the nothingness of an abstractly asserted, absolute trueness. The passion for truth of assertion is turned into the passion for truth of denying. Then there arises the scrupulosity of the fanatic for truth, who can no longer grasp any truth, but is endlessly on the move, without ever reaching a decision. The untruthfulness of his action shows itself in the pretense of surpassing exactitude in truth, through which in fact he renders himself incapable of grasping truth. It permits him, out of his own not-being, to be able to negate all that is positive, lived, done, grasped in the other person.[2]

"SATAN'S TRUTH" (ACCORDING TO DIETRICH BONHOEFFER)

Every word I utter is subject to the requirement that it shall be true. Quite apart from the veracity of its contents, the relation between myself and another man which is expressed in it is in itself either true or untrue. I can speak flatteringly or presumptuously or hypocritically without uttering a material untruth; yet my words are nevertheless untrue, because I am disrupting and destroying the reality of the relationship between man and wife, superior and subordinate, etc. An individual utterance is always part of a total reality which seeks expression in this utterance. If my utterance is to be truthful it must in each case be different according to whom I am addressing, who is questioning me, and what I am speaking about. The truthful word is not in itself constant; it is as much alive as life itself. If it is detached from life and from its reference to the concrete other man, if "the truth is told" without taking into account to whom it is addressed, then this truth has only the appearance of truth, but it lacks its essential character.

It is only the cynic who claims "to speak the truth" at all times and in all places to all men in the same way, but who, in fact, displays nothing but a lifeless image of the truth. He dons the halo of the fanatical devotee of truth who can make no allowance for human weaknesses; but, in fact, he is destroying the living truth between men. He wounds shame, desecrates mystery, breaks confidence, betrays the community in which he lives, and laughs arrogantly at the devastation he has wrought and at the human weakness which "cannot bear the truth." He says truth is destructive and demands its victims, and he feels like a god above these feeble creatures and does not know that he is serving Satan.

There is a truth which is of Satan. Its essence is that under the semblance of truth it denies everything that is real. It lives upon hatred of the real and of the world which is created and loved by God. It pretends to be executing the judgment of God upon the fall of the real. God's truth judges created things out of love, and Satan's truth judges them out of envy and hatred. God's truth has become flesh in the world and is alive in the real, but Satan's truth is the death of all reality.

The concept of living truth is dangerous, and it gives rise to the suspicion that the truth can and may be adapted to each particular situation in a way which completely destroys the idea of truth and narrows the gap between truth and falsehood, so that the two become indistinguishable. Moreover, what we are saying about the necessity for discerning the real may be mistakenly understood as meaning that it is by adopting a calculating or schoolmasterly attitude towards the other man that I shall decide what proportion of the truth I am prepared to tell him. It is important that this danger should be kept in view. Yet the only possible way of countering it is by means of attentive discernment of the particular contents and limits which the real itself imposes on one's utterance in order to make it a truthful one. The dangers which are involved in the concept of living truth must never impel one to abandon this concept in favor of the formal and cynical concept of truth.[3]

THE SERVICE OF THEOLOGY (ACCORDING TO KARL BARTH)

Theology in the form which mainly occupies us here is related to the community and its faith in roughly the same manner as jurisprudence is related to the state and its law. The inquiry and doctrine of theology, therefore, are not an end in themselves but, rather, functions of the community and especially of its *ministerium Verbi Divini*. Theology is committed directly to the community and especially to those members who are responsible for preaching, teaching and counseling. The task theology has to fulfil is continually to stimulate and lead them to face squarely the question of the proper relation of their human speech to the Word of God, which is the origin, object, and content of this speech. Theology must give them practice in the right relation to the quest for truth, demonstrating and exemplifying to them the understanding, thought, and discourse proper to it. It must accustom them to the fact that here nothing can be taken for granted, that work, just as prayer, is indispensable. It also has the task of exhibiting the lines along which this work is to be conducted.

Theology would be an utter failure if it should place itself in some elegant eminence where it would be concerned only with God, the world, man, and some other items, perhaps those of historical interest, instead of being theology for the *community*. Like the pendulum which regulates the movements of a clock, so theology is responsible for the reasonable service of the community. It reminds all its members, especially those who have greater responsibilities, how serious is their situation and task. In this way it opens for them the way to freedom and joy in their service.

But in order to serve the community of *today*, theology itself must be rooted in the community of *yesterday*. *Its* testimony to the Word and the profession of *its* faith must originate, like the community itself, from the community *of past times*, from which that of today arose. Theology must originate also from the older and the more recent *tradition* which determines the present form of its witness. The foundation of its inquiry and instruction is given to theology beforehand, along with the task which it has to fulfil. Theology does not labor somewhere high above the foundation of tradition, as though Church history began today. Nevertheless, the special task of theology is a *critical* one, in spite of its relative character. The fire of the *quest for truth* has to ignite the proclamation of the community and the tradition determining this proclamation. Theology has to reconsider the confession of the community, testing and rethinking it in the light of its enduring foundation, object, and content.

The faith of the community is asked to seek understanding. Faith seeking understanding, *Fides quaerens intellectum*, is what theology must embody and represent. What distinguishes faith from blind assent is just its special character as "faith seeking understanding." Certainly, the assumption behind all this will be that the community itself may have been on the right track in the recent or remote past, or at any rate on a not altogether crooked path. Consequently fundamental trust instead of mistrust will be the initial attitude of theology toward the tradition which determines the present-day Church. And any questions and proposals which theology has to direct to the tradition will definitely not be forced on the community like a decree; any such findings will be presented for consideration only as well-weighed suggestions. Nevertheless, no ecclesiastical authority should be allowed by theology to hinder it from honestly pursuing its critical task, and the same applies to any frightened voices from the midst of the rest of the congregation. The task of theology is to discuss freely the reservations as well as the proposals for improvement which occur to it in reflection on the inherited witness of the community. Theology says *credo*, I believe, along with the present-day community and its fathers. But it says *credo ut intelligam*, "I believe in order to understand." To achieve this understanding, it must be granted leeway for the good of the community itself.[4]

What we would like to see is an open, broad Protestant Church, capable of communication and capable of contact, from whose truthfulness the Catholic Church can learn, since it is lived in truth. A Protestant Church, therefore, which listens and permits others to talk with her, which speaks, lives and then—when necessary—also protests in the light of positive reality, but which also raises questions about herself and has no fixed judgment on the other Church of which she constantly has to assure herself. A Protestant Church above all which in relation to the Catholic Church is wholly truthful in the truth, without fear, without thought of prestige, without constriction in exclusiveness; a Church then engaged—also and particularly with the Catholic Church—in the positive realization of Christendom.

Immediately after the announcement of the Council, almost ten years ago, the author of the present book published a book on the Council and Reunion ("Renewal as a Call to Unity")[5] in which an attempt was made to provide a brief list of the main Protestant demands to the Catholic Church and to make them intelligible and fruitful for the Council. A later chapter in the present book will show how much of what was of concern to the Protestants has already been adopted in the Catholic Church. What has astonished the author of that earlier book is that it has *up to now* had no counterpart in which, soberly and without any "catholicizing," a list of the justified Catholic concerns in the light of the gospel in relation to the Evangelical Church would be provided and substantiated by a competent, authoritative Evangelical theologian.

NOTES

1. F. Lau, *Luther* (Berlin, 1959), pp. 140f.; quoted from *Luther* by Franz Lau, translated by Robert H. Fischer. The Westminster Press. Copyright © 1963 by W. L. Jenkins. Used by permission.
2. K. Jaspers, *Von der Wahrheit* (Munich, 1958²), pp. 560f.
3. D. Bonhoeffer, *Ethik*, zusammengestellt und herausgegeben von E. Bethge (Munich, 1961⁵), pp. 284f.; quoted from *Ethics*, ed. Eberhard Bethge, trans. Neville Horton Smith (New York, Macmillan, paper, 1965), pp. 365-367. Reprinted with permission of the Macmillan Company. Copyright 1955 by SCM Press.
4. K. Barth, *Einführung in die evangelische Theologie* (Zurich, 1962), pp. 49-52; quoted from *Evangelical Theology*, trans. by Grover Foley (New York, Doubleday Anchor Book, 1964), pp. 35-37. Copyright © 1963 by Karl Barth. Reprinted by permission of Holt, Rinehart and Winston, Inc.
5. *The Council, Reform and Reunion*, trans. Cecily Hastings (New York, Sheed and Ward, 1961).

IV/Institutional Church—Obstacle to Truthful Christian Existence?

IS THE CHURCH really credible? The Church must be worthy of belief. Faith is certainly not an act of reason to be compelled by rational evidence, but neither is it an irrational act of violence on the part of the will. Christian faith, precisely because it is God's gift, is not a blind "intellectual sacrifice" in which man offers to God, or even to the Church, the sacrifice of his understanding. Christian faith is the intelligent commitment of the whole man, which does not exclude but presupposes rational thinking. Faith is corrupted when it becomes intellectually dishonest, when—that is —it suppresses, forgets, shuts out genuine rational difficulties as illegitimate doubts, instead of facing up to them with complete truthfulness. Anyway, the "solution" of these difficulties does not always depend on the believing subject; the "object" to be believed and its credibility are also involved. In the concrete: a Church which has become incredible renders difficult or—in the individual case—even impossible a truthful *Credo ecclesiam*, a faith in God *in the Church*.

To be sure, an individual believer may occasionally apply to the Church—to this community of human beings, and sinful human beings—standards which are too narrow and too strict, to which he himself could scarcely measure up. But this is far from saying that too much is always demanded. Must it, then, not have something to do with the Church, her concrete situation and her defects, that numbers of devout Christians—by no means individualistic lone wolves in splendid isolation, but the kind who very readily think with a community, co-operate in a common task, indeed want to incorporate their thought into the thought of a community of believers—feel repelled by the "institutional" Church as it is now and thus prefer to be truthfully Christian outside the Church? For the sake of truthfulness they set themselves apart from this Church by leaving under protest or by silently withdrawing into the inner emigration. Must we suppose all these people have acted in this way merely because of ignorance or vexation? or has not the Church in the concrete provided at least the occasion for their action? Can a Christian not simply feel that his *Credo ecclesiam* demands too much of him in a wholly concrete situation involving the Church and himself?

Is the Church, then, credible? Does she help men to be truthfully Christian, to be truthfully human? Some maintain that she is rather an obstacle to this, by which they mean, not the Church as a community of persons, as a community of believers, but in fact the Church as an institution, an institutional system, an institutional structure. This Church would indeed unhesitatingly sacrifice truth over and over again to ecclesiastical authority—which must under no circumstances be diminished or jeopardized—and surrender persons to institutions. This Church is concerned less with the message of the gospel and the welfare of men than with her antiquated, rigid institutions, her frequently obsolete, unrealistic constitutions, her over-cherished authority, her dead system. And the consequence is uncertainty, fear, dread, and the enslavement of men by an institutional regime that is intolerant, indifferent in the last resort to the concrete needs and concerns of concrete human beings, and in reality unloving. As the latest, particularly devastating example of this the treatment of the question of birth control is frequently cited, as showing quite clearly that truth has been sacrificed to the prestige of the Church's magisterium, and human need to concern for the institution.

The complex of problems cannot be examined in its whole extent in the space at our disposal. Here, on the question of the institutional Church as such, the attempt will be made only to set forth certain comments, which do not solve the problem but show what is really important: the first three, negative; the second three, positive.

1. It is impossible to justify the present institutional ecclesiastical system simply by an appeal to the very popular and very worn-out concept of "development." There are limits to the elasticity of this concept and to the credibility of its application. In fact, not every "development" in constitution and doctrine—the question of development of dogma will be dealt with expressly later —can be substantiated from Scripture. In theology too the concept of evolution must not be understood in an idealistic-romantic fashion.

Precisely from the theological standpoint a first factor must be recognized. There is in principle—since it is a question of a Church consisting of men, and sinful men—in the expansion of the institutional system in doctrine and constitution also an *evolutio contra evangelium,* unevangelical development, real faulty development. In this is included all that transgresses the message of Christ and particularly what suppresses and destroys the truthfulness, freedom and humanity of the children of God. Such a development in the Church may *in no case even be merely tolerated.*

And secondly there is in principle in the expansion of the institutional system also an *evolutio praeter evangelium,* an extra-evangelical, actual development alongside the gospel which, even if it is not forbidden by the gospel, is at any rate not authorized by it. This includes everything that is not laid down in the message of Christ, but has in fact prevailed as a result of other influences in the Church. Such a "development" may be tolerated in the Church, although only in the light of the circumstances at the time, and therefore certainly *in no case turned into an absolute.*

2. It is impossible to find an adequate biblical basis for what is called the "*Roman* system" (and which, for Catholic theologians, is identical neither with the Catholic Church nor with a Petrine office in the Church). In this connection there is much that does not need

to be theologically substantiated, but must be explained mainly by political and social factors.

In fact, this "Roman system"—so far as it means the liturgical, theological and administrative centralism and juridicism which is receding today, so far as it means the authoritarianism, absolutism and imperialism of the Roman Curia, criticized on all sides today— was, particularly after the "Constantinian turning point," more and more clearly in the making, but it prevailed in the Latin Church only in the high Middle Ages after the Gregorian reform, and from then on was methodically expanded, although with frequent reverses, up to the time between the two Vatican Councils. We have examined elsewhere in both its exegetical-historical and systematic theological aspects, as well as the practical-pastoral, the very complex question of the Petrine office in the Church.[1]

3. It is impossible to find an adequate biblical basis for all the features of the present constitution of the Church (even apart from the "Roman system") which are in fact important. Much of what is expounded in the third chapter of the Constitution on the Church in regard to offices in the Church does not belong from the beginning, and in this essentially, to the Church but is a matter of historical development on which the most diverse factors had an influence. This would include the three-office arrangement, normal from the time of Ignatius of Antioch, and especially the distinction —not only jurisdictional but quasi-dogmatic—between bishops and presbyters and the present circumscription of the diverse functions of office (also that of the deacons); further, much of what is actually more a sociological than a theological demarcation between clergy and laity, between office and community; finally, by far the greater part of the codification of Canon Law.[2] For all this the principle holds: what does not exist in its essentials from the origin of the Church may not be turned into an absolute, but is in principle open to change.

If the content of the above three comments were to be taken seriously in theory and practice in the Catholic Church, a large part of the contemporary objections to the "institutional Church" would lose their force. Then truthful existence in the Church and truthful existence of the Church would be possible in quite another fashion. And yet these three negative comments envisage only the one aspect of the problem-complex. They must be considered together with three positive comments which attempt to investigate the other aspect and which may indicate why so many Catholics who adopt a highly critical attitude towards the institutional ecclesiastical system *remain* in this concrete Church, certainly suffering under all the human weaknesses, shortcomings and illnesses, defects and errors, of this system and yet in unclouded clarity of vision and sincerity, with strong hope and by no means without joy.

1. The Church could not continue without the institutional factor. Even charismatics must admit this if they do not want to become utopian fanatics. The equivocal concept of "institution" or "institutional Church" is frequently used in an absolutely vague, undifferentiated sense. Is this the same as ecclesiastical "system," "structure," "organization," or again as "official Church," "hierarchy," her constitution and her dogma? Moreover, is everything in the dogma and constitution of the Catholic Church "institutional" in the negative sense? Or is there also something "institutional," "appointed," in the positive sense?

Is the Church as a community of believers, as a *congregatio fidelium,* not also at the same time *institutio Dei,* God's planting, foundation? And is not therefore something simply "given," "appointed," "instituted" from the origin of the Church, something indeed which must be ever freshly accepted, grasped, realized by the faithful, but which just so is not left to their whim, to their action or inaction, for them to do in one way or another? Are we not aware, precisely from the biblical message, of decisive elements which must indeed be constantly shaped anew by the believing community in concrete historicity, but which as such are at the same time present in advance in a definite although open ground-plan not itself under the control of the ecclesial community and the individual believer?

Does this not hold for the gospel message itself and also for baptism, the Eucharist and certain basic features of Church order (charismatic structure, priesthood of all believers, special ministries

with special authority within the community)? Is not God's will
expressly manifested in these things according to the New Testament, even though a formal act of institution is not always exegetic-
ally-historically demonstrable? Do not precisely these "ordinances"
—which demand obedient fulfilment in the spirit of Christ—impose
a special responsibility on men? Are the order of the worship and
the order of the life of the Church conceivable without "institutional" elements in the broadest sense? Is it not precisely through
this that man and the human community—which would otherwise
be loaded with excessive burdens—in the realization of their Christian existence are permanently relieved of the necessity of constantly starting out again from the very beginning and of fashioning
everything anew from the start?

In short: Can we simply reject an "institutional" Church? Would
we not have to distinguish between "institution" and "institutionalism," between good and bad, between a permanently necessary
and relative-transitory institution, between an "institutional" and
"institutionalist" Church? Might we not therefore in a differentiated
judgment certainly reject in fact a particular institutional structure,
expansion, superstructure of the Catholic Church, which had come
to be historically and has now outlived its time, but not simply the
"institutional Church"? The latter means leaving the Church, which
can certainly shock but rarely change much in the Church; the
former means criticism in the Church, which can move the seem-
ingly immovable.

2. There is in the Church also development in accordance with
the gospel. A considerable part of what has developed in the two
thousand years of history of the Catholic Church is *evolutio praeter
evangelium*: a purely factual historical development, not authorized by the gospel, which *can* disappear again. Or it is even an
evolutio contra evangelium: an unevangelical, unchristian, faulty
development, which *must* disappear again. But together and frequently mingled with all this there is also *evolutio secundum
evangelium*: a development in accordance with the gospel, required
by the gospel, the legitimate and frequently factually necessary
development of the origin in a new age.

Such a development—and perhaps the one richest in consequences—is already found in the New Testament itself: the translation of the gospel message into a new world through the hellenistic
communities, through Paul and John; the creeds already being
formed or accepted in the New Testament epistles; the development and transformation of the conception of baptism and the
Eucharist; the development and then the blending of the Palestinian
and the Pauline constitution of the Church, and so on. Consequently it is possible to find fault only with the unwarranted
extension and incredible application of the conception of development, not with the concept itself. In theory and practice we shall
have to examine very closely what is *contra, praeter* or *secundum*
of the criticism so widespread today of the institutionalist Church,
evangelium: what is required, permitted or forbidden by the gospel;
what is development contrary to the gospel, apart from the gospel
or according to the gospel; what therefore must be abolished, can
be tolerated or may be approved.

3. There is in the Church a reform of institutions. A large part
also and particularly of the hierarchy, also and quite particularly
of Rome, must be recognized as justified. What is more, things must
not remain so. If ever there was a time when we could say it with
well-founded hope, then it is in the great upheaval of the Church
today: things will not remain so. The principle, *ecclesia semper
reformanda*, which obtained through the Council an unexpected
theoretical as well as practical recognition, aims not only at the individual and a "reform of persons," but also and primarily at the
Church as such and at a "reform of institutions." Certainly,
opinions are divided in our Church about the radicality of these reforms. But every Christian and particularly every theologian has
the great chance today of applying himself *in* the Church with all
his strength to the reform which he knows to be necessary in the
light of the original Christian message and of the changed times.

Even Chapter 3 of the Constitution on the Church, on the
hierarchy, both exegetically and historically highly problematic—
for many a critic this world of juridical functions, very different
from that of the first two chapters, is derived more from a rigid

feudalism than from the message of the gospel—even this does not in principle close any doors. This is not merely an ecumenically inspired pious wish. We should not overlook the fact that, from the standpoint of modern exegetical-historical studies, this chapter analyzes, not the permanent historical *essence* of the ecclesial ministries, decisively determined by its origin, but only a very *time-conditioned* historical *manifestation* of the offices. Only to a person skilled in exegesis and history, perhaps, was its meaning clear in its whole import. This chapter does not claim to give an exegetically and historically substantiated exposition based on origins. But it provides a theological-pastoral description of the nature, order and function of the diverse offices oriented to the *present* order of the Church. The theological commission itself, in its commentary on the third chapter, observes on the three-office order: "Whatever may be the historical origin of presbyters, deacons, or other ministries and also the exact sense of the terms used to designate them in the New Testament, it is affirmed . . ."

This means that the real theological work in the *light of the New Testament* and of *historical development* is still to be accomplished.[3] The results will doubtless provide us with a new freedom in regard to the solidity, rigidity and overemphasis of the present "hierarchical structure," which have come about historically. The Council itself has initiated the theoretical reconsideration and practical reorganization, of which all the consequences cannot yet be foreseen.

Some are sceptical. But even sceptics sometimes deceive themselves. And how often have the prophets of doom within and without the Church been found wrong when they asserted that this or that reform was not possible in theory or practice; that this or that element could not be assimilated, integrated, modified; that the Catholic Church then would no longer be the Catholic Church; then it would have an essentially different structure, it would lose its identity, and so on.

Certainly there arise supremely difficult problems of continuity or discontinuity of teaching and practice. But do we want *a priori* to forbid the Catholic Church a radical *metanoia*? In a Church to which doom has been already prophesied so often in two thousand years, and always mistakenly, there is room for hope. Anyway, Christian hope does not mean any sort of feeble passivity. There is no reform without struggle; no renewal without controversy. A sick person is not helped by theory alone. If the Church sincerely wants to have a new future, then the *ecclesia semper reformanda* must not become dead truth: rather must it become living reality.

NOTES

1. Cf. *The Church,* E II, 3.
2. The exegetical-historical evidence for these perhaps apparently bold observations is to be found in the work cited above, *The Church,* E II, 2.
3. This is the perspective in which our book *The Church* must be seen.

V/Truthfulness in Practical Reform

ANYONE WHO makes a positive effort to gain a theological understanding of the Church in her indispensable external structures has more right than the critical outsider to say that all theoretical elucidation in regard to the "institutional Church" is of little use if the factual accomplishment, the practical realization in the concrete Church, does not correspond to it. This in fact, wholly apart from theoretical and particularly exegetical-historical difficulties, is for very many the root of their rejection of an "institutional Church": the painful existential experience of the concrete Church, which can lead to a growing aversion from this Church.

Certainly it is possible to have other, more positive, experiences than its numerous critics with the "institutional Church": we shall return to this. Nevertheless, does not anyone with even a little insight into the concrete life of the Church know how much is true —in spite of everything—in the accusations against an "institutional Church," which constantly and mercilessly disregards human beings, injures them, is able indeed almost to cripple them? Even in our century cannot innumerable examples be given, even apart from the "more famous" cases in the anti-Modernist dispute or those under Pius XII, like the worker-priests, the purge of theologians in France, and other victims of the ecclesiastical inquisition in the twentieth century [1] (and also not a few signs of the continued existence of the spirit of the Roman Inquisition even after the post-conciliar reform of that institution)? Who does not recall all the innumerable dismissals and removals, prohibitions on writing and speaking; the practice of concealment and of denunciations; all the condemnations without a hearing, the multiplicity of disciplinary measures, the chicanery—small and great—to which particularly theologians, parish priests, curates, religious—even in the dioceses—have been exposed; the scarcely democratic procedure for appointments to office in the Church (election of bishops, occupation of parishes), and so on? But who does not think also of matters affecting the laity: suppression of free discussion, abuses in regard to marriage cases, unnecessary imposition of burdens, Church commandments, decrees, directives; the harsh, unintelligent, doctrinaire answers given to so many real-life questions—on the question of Catholic schools, of marital morality, of ecumenical co-operation?

How often, without anyone directly intending it, is the impersonal system in fact placed (by really good men) above persons, their dignity and rights? How many of the "little people" have often had to suffer in this respect who ought not to have had to suffer; how many consciences have been burdened which ought to have been free and joyous; how many creative minds in the parishes, in the dioceses, in the Church as a whole, have been paralyzed; how many precious initiatives have been suppressed, or the action they gave rise to subsequently brought to a halt? How much that was good has always had to be established in the Church, in the beginning, against the wishes of the hierarchy? How much fear, hypocrisy, discouragement, immaturity, inactivity, in the lower ranks of the Church; how much fear and insecurity, prejudice and incompetence, and thence—not through malice—intolerance, passivity and uncharitableness in the higher ranks? All at the expense of truthful Christian existence in a truthful Church.

No. At this point it will be better not to contradict the critics. Certainly all this is not the whole Church for us; it is not the good nature, but the evil un-nature of the Church. Other things are very much more important. But it ought to be admitted: there is *also* all this in the Church, this very dark un-nature of the Church. For anyone who knows this the facts speak a harsh and clear language. Nor should it be said that all this has been involved from the very beginning in the feebleness and wretchedness of this Church of men and Church of sinners. It is not as simple as this. Much of what has been mentioned exists only when—and as long as—that structure and expansion of an ecclesiastical apparatus of power exists which is oriented more to its own authority and prestige than to the message of the gospel and to men, which even today retains some amazingly Byzantine, medieval and modern-absolutist features. Almost nowhere so clearly as in the Church is the sociological law of the cumulative effect of the institution manifested: the already existing institutions produce new ones.

In order to avoid the impression that apologetics is here being turned into an apologia and that the problem could be solved by words alone, our answer will be quite short. Two things are necessary:

1. An honest, truthful examination of conscience, linked with an historical reflection on the failures of the "institutional Church" in the last decades: for instance, in regard to Nazism, Fascism, the Jews, the race question, war, etc., where the Church all too often has compromised her mission for the sake of institutional positions.

2. A truthful, practical change. The Church and her institutions must again be oriented afresh to service to men in a transformed historical situation. All institutions and constitutions must serve persons. Instead of making myths out of historically emerging institutions, under the spell of a theological conservatism, they must be constantly renewed in elastic adaptation to the transformation of the social structure. In the Church too the historically correct legal system must constantly be rediscovered. There must be neither positivistic relativization nor dogmatic fixation of the institutional factor. A spiritless statism leads to the decay of the institution: only a spirited, responsible dynamism keeps it alive.

Hence it is primarily for the responsible ministers of the Church in church government and theology, everywhere and at all levels, resolutely and energetically to take in hand the necessary reforms, and even in "ecclesiastical politics" and decisions on everyday matters in the Church—as already frequently happens—to make the message of Jesus prevail in a new fashion. Guided by the gospel of Jesus Christ, we must overcome fears and uncertainties, break down ideological fanaticism and resentful narrow-mindedness, loosen constriction and petrifaction

Certainly, the authorities everywhere in human society love the status quo, often even the *status quo ante*. They are averse to radical changes, which mean considerable unpleasantness and inconvenience: they are in possession and might lose something; often (not always) reforms are a question of generations; sometimes death alone succeeds in solving certain problems of reform which involve personalities. But one way or another, people today are looking for a truthful Church of the future, in whose structures, in whose institutions and constitutions, truth is not manipulated, the word not diluted, the spirit not canalized, life not stifled, freedom not despised, justice not suppressed, peace not broken. This means discussion instead of denunciation, comprehension instead of inquisition, communication instead of excommunication, mental expansion instead of mental frustration. It means dialogue instead of dictation, criticism instead of censorship, frankness instead of concealment, trust in the truth instead of branding people as heretics.

Thus the absolutist, authoritarian and often totalitarian system must give way to genuine order in freedom, hierarchical power to ecclesial service, clerical despotism to spiritual leadership, narrow-mindedness and reserve to openness towards all reality, fear of freedom to courage for commitment, mistrust to honest co-operation, cherished dependency to Christian maturity. Not sluggish routine, but inventive initiative; not outward fuss, but inward conviction; not faint-heartedness, but faith; not hidebound narrow-mindedness, but the broad horizon of the world. There is no need of obedient church functionaries and servants of the system, for whose selection conformity with the official party line is the supreme criterion; for whom—in spite of all personal integrity— paternalistic one-man rule, legalistic morality and canonistic narrow-mindedness, both bureaucratic insensitivity towards concrete persons and needs and intolerance towards deviating opinions, are characteristic.

Such hierarchs (and sometimes hierarchesses too) are largely responsible if still more priests and religious—men and women— leave the Church disappointed and if the Church for so many seems anything but a home of truthfulness. The need is rather for men in the Church—who are very much more numerous today—who are whole men and as such servants of their fellow-men: lovable and relaxed, modest and superior, enjoying risk and conscious of responsibility; thinking fraternally instead of paternally, in terms of partnership instead of hierarchically; for whom laws exist for the sake of men and not conversely; for whom the great tradition points forward; who do not avoid consultation and discussion, but seek it and draw the people concerned into the decision-making process; who in every case decide in the light of the requirements of the gospel and of the time, and who thus display the bold energy of the deed at the service of a radical renewal.

Anyone who wants the Church to die out, to become the grave of God, must want her to remain as she is. Anyone who wants her to live, as God's living congregation, must want her to change. Only by changing does she remain what she is. Only by renewal is she preserved. Would not this be a Church truthful in quite another way, making it not more difficult but easier for anyone who would like to be truthfully a Christian: not an encapsulated religious association, appearing to the outsider as alien, exclusive, unapproachable, but an unprejudiced, wide-open, richly differentiated, mobile-lively, hospitable community?

Such a Church would certainly not dissolve into disparate, unorganized groups. She could not avoid being organized and unified in the pluralist society: if an organization *alongside* others is wanted. But such a Church would at the same time operate *in* all others through the human beings who are active, filled with the message and spirit of Christ: the salt of the earth and the light of the world in modern life. And therefore this Church, in spite of her (also) institutional character, would not be a party monopoly, a uniform army, a monolithic block, an absolutist-religious *Imper-*

ium Romanum. She would allow scope for initiative, she would encourage small groups to operate as committed in an unconventional way in the secular world and to experiment without being officially controlled in everything: manifold cells in the diverse spheres of life, fraternally united with their fellow-men; teams courageously advancing into the most varied country, involved in the ordinary concerns of the world, not wanting to rule but to help, thus complementing the institutional Church in a necessary way (as the religious orders originally did), broadening, vivifying it, making it mobile and communicative in an extraordinary way.

The signs of the times today point in this direction: in the Church there will be again—the future has already begun—more truthfulness, freedom, humanity, more broadmindedness, tolerance, magnanimity, more Christian self-confidence, more sovereign patience, more courage for thought and decision, and with all this more joy, happiness, true peace and unshakable hope. This Church will not be constantly behind her time, but as much as possible in advance of it: a true and truthful Church of the future.

NOTES

1. To give only one concrete example. This is what we are told of Pierre Teilhard de Chardin. In 1926 his superiors withdrew him from his chair at the Institut Catholique in Paris. In 1927 the Roman censors refused an *imprimatur* for *Le milieu divin*. In 1933 the Roman superiors forbade him any activity in Paris. In 1938 he was forbidden to publish *L'Energie Humaine*. In 1944 the censors rejected his chief work, *Le Phénomène Humaine*. In 1947 he was directed by his superiors not to deal any longer with philosophical themes. In 1948 he was forbidden to accept a call to the Collège de France. In 1949 the censors rejected *Le Group Zoologique Humain*. In 1951 he was "exiled" from Europe to the research institute of the Wenner-Gren foundation in New York. In 1954 he stayed for two months on a visit to Paris, but had to leave the city hastily six weeks before the date he had intended because of Roman hostility. In the year of his death, 1955, he was forbidden to take part in the international congress of palaeontologists. A single person followed his coffin when Teilhard was buried on Easter Sunday around a hundred miles from New York.

The list of works drawn up by C. Cuénot certainly amounts to 380. Teilhard, however, was allowed to publish only purely specialized scientific works. During his lifetime he had no opportunity to see even one of his major works in print. After his death, with the Order's permission, the ownership of his manuscripts was bequeathed to his secretary Jeanne Mortier and was thus withdrawn from the sphere of influence of the Roman censors. How this theologian might have been able to work if his obedience to the Church had not been so outrageously abused and he had been allowed to go on working. And how much might his scientific work have gained—losing at the same time some of its lack of balance—if it had been constantly exposed to public criticism.

VI/The Beginning of a Change

WE ARE still far from the goal, from a goal which *a priori* we can only approach, which we can never gain. A great, gigantic task, but today it is being seen, discovered, measured in a new way. Christians, including many good and far-seeing, responsible members of the Church's ministry at all levels, have taken a new interest in it. We must not act as if nothing decisive had yet occurred. There is not the slightest occasion for defeatism. The Church—the constantly failing and straying Church certainly—is in spite of all on the way, the good way on which John XXIII shows how much can be set in motion under often relatively slight, spontaneous impulses. And, in spite of all failures, the Council—as we begin to perceive in the often very rapid post-conciliar development still more clearly than during the Council—has initiated a quite fundamental change, which has already brought innumerable fruits in the concrete life of men: in the interior life of the Church, in relations with other Christians and Christian Churches, in relations with the Jews and the great world-religions, in regard to the modern world altogether.

Not the least important evidence of this is provided by the present signs of crisis, which may be signs of a new birth. The fact cannot be overlooked that, in spite of all delays, the work of reforming institutions is also being put in hand in the post-conciliar age: reforms in worship, abolition of unnecessary fasting regulations, abolition of the Index and other inquisitorial measures, abolition of inopportune ecclesiastical prohibitions (such as that on cremation), new occupants for curial posts, and so on. For some, who are strongly rooted in the Catholic tradition, progress today is not too slow, but rather too rapid. Anyway, we need patience *and* impatience at once. It is precisely out of suffering through the Church that action for the Church will be born. And the Church, which succeeded in emerging out of the wretchedness of Renaissance times, will also master the difficulties of today which are differently situated. It is a grand thing for those who are permitted to work together *in* the Church at the beginning of a new epoch.

And it is a question of a new epoch, of the beginning of an epochal change. As John XXIII became a transitional pope in an unexpected sense of the word, and the Second Vatican Council a transitional council, so is the Catholic Church today altogether a transitional Church: transition from a past that has by no means passed away into a future only just arriving. A complex and sometimes contradictory process, liberating for the great number inside and outside the Catholic Church, depressing too for some within the Church: at any rate we are still in the midst of the process. It will take some decades at least for the true historical importance of Vatican II to become visible.

Who would have thought at the time that the insignificant Council of Trent, which was attended for the most part only by some dozens of Italian and Spanish bishops, would give its name to a period of four hundred years, a period that we now so often describe as having come to an end. By comparison with the post-Tridentine, Counter-Reformation Church, the Second Vatican Council—with all the half-measures that we must never conceal —means in its basic trend a turning of 180°. Certainly, it is still the same Church and it must remain the same. And yet it is a new Church that has emerged from the Second Vatican Council.

What matter are the basic tendencies, which are certainly still far from being consistently realized; these may be set out in a series of contrasts. Then—in the post-Reformation, post-Tridentine age —introversion and concentration of the Catholic Church on herself; now an opening out towards others. Then condemnation and excommunication of those who held different beliefs; now conversation, dialogue with them. Then rejection of any serious, official self-criticism; now from Pope and Council a confession of guilt and of many a faulty development. Then the idealistic affirmation of a Church without spot or wrinkle; now demand for a comprehensive reform and renewal. Then self-righteous summoning of heretics and schismatics to return; now ecumenical encounter with the brethren in Christ and with other Christian Churches; and increasing realization of their claims. Then splendid isolation from the modern world; now understanding dialogue with the modern world and with modern man outside the Church. Then people extolled the monolithic unity, power and solidarity of the Catholic body; now they demand emergence from the ghetto and the breaking down of many barriers. Then people admired the massive legal structure and rigid organization of the Catholic Church; now they react against juridicism and demand interiorization. Then personal cult was offered to ecclesiastical office-holders of all grades; now there is opposition to clericalism and a demand for the fraternity of all Christians and for ecclesiastical office as service to the brethren. Then the Church was deified as a perfect, divine-human reality between heaven and earth, which could be identified with the kingdom of God; now there is opposition to triumphalism and a demand for the Christian realism which sees the Church as a Church of human beings, and sinful human beings, as the pilgrim people of God moving through the darkness of sin and error towards the future kingdom of God.

The new basic tendencies, shifts of emphasis, intentions, objectives, are well-known. But what was achieved in the concrete? It is a great pity that the Council did not solve three problems which seem particularly important to the man in the street: birth control, mixed marriages, reform of the Roman Curia. The result is that the other positive results—which are not at once directly visible—are far from being known as well as they deserve to be. And yet what was achieved is essential as a basis for the future. For that reason we shall attempt here to make a provisional inventory of the results of the Council—with a glance at the Church of the future. Appreciation of the results varies very much with different observers. Here we shall attempt simply a résumé from the inner-Catholic, indeed inner-conciliar standpoint, but with an outward view directed to Christendom and to the world. In spite of all justifiable criticism, people will certainly not interpret it as apologetic window-dressing if, now that the Council has closed, we bring out first of all the positive achievements. It is certainly too simple to say: in the preparation of the Council's decrees a realistic pessimism, in their execution a realistic optimism. But there is some truth in this. What was not achieved need not and—for the sake of truthfulness—must not by any means be overlooked.

There are certain decrees (e.g., the decree on mass media, the declaration on Christian education) which contain scarcely anything referring to the future. There are others which are very unbalanced, ambiguous at some points and at others backward-looking. There is perhaps no decree at all which entirely satisfied bishops and theologians. Almost everywhere, particularly in the doctrinal decrees (the almost total absence of Catholic exegetes in the Council has had serious consequences), there is lacking a solid exegetical, and often too a solid historical, basis. Frequently, precisely the most difficult points (e.g., Scripture-Tradition, primacy-collegiality, etc.) were pasted over with diplomatic compromises: between a Council majority, which generally had serious and lively theology on its side, and the relatively small curial party, which had on its side the power of the machinery in the commissions and exploited this right to the end with impressive boldness and untiring energy.

None of this should be concealed at all. The episcopate, theology and the whole Church will have to make sure that they do not subsequently lose much of what has been achieved, through the workings of a cold bureaucracy. And the theology of the post-conciliar age certainly has its hands full in interpreting, clarifying, and also constantly making fresh corrections with absolutely honest and critical theological objectivity. But, in spite of everything, it is important now, first of all, not to lament the indisputable obscurities, compromises, omissions, one-sidedness, setbacks and mistakes, as defects of the past, but, with forward-looking hope, to face them as *tasks of the future*: in the spirit of the Council, which did not want to close any doors. Indeed, the Council, the true realization of the Council-Event, in a sense *began* on the eighth of December, 1965. And precisely in order to prepare the better future, we must at present not allow the better to be the enemy of the good, but permit the good to be the herald of better things.

We ask then: Where are the doors opened? Where are the gleams of light? In the stream of the Council, among all the historical detritus, sand and pebbles, which have inevitably been carried along from a two-thousand-year-old history, where do we find the gold which if we are able to do something with it—will bring rewards in the future? With the aid of the sixteen different Council documents, our survey will be directed to this end.

A. THE ECUMENICAL AGE

What on the whole has the Council achieved in regard to other Christians? The decree on Ecumenism particularly means that something decisive has occurred.

1. The Catholic share of the guilt of schism is acknowledged in every way and a plea for pardon was addressed to the other Christians by both Council and Pope. At the same time the necessity of constant reform was recognized: *ecclesia semper reformanda*— renewal of our own Church in life and doctrine according to the gospel.

2. The other Christian communities are recognized as Churches. Formerly only individuals were acknowledged ("heretics," "schismatics"); now communities are recognized. And in fact they are addressed, not as any sort of community, but as ecclesial communities, or Churches. There is in all Churches a common Christian basis that is perhaps more important than all that divides us.

3. An ecumenical attitude is required from the whole Church: inner conversion of Catholics themselves and prayer in an ecumenical spirit; then the Churches' coming to know one another in

understanding dialogue; recognition of the good in others and learning from them; recognition of the faith, the charity, the baptism of other Christians; finally, the study of theology and Church history pursued in an ecumenical spirit.

4. Co-operation with other Christians is to be promoted in every way. Practical co-operation is possible in the whole social field. But prayer in common, too, is desirable (John XXIII was the first pope to pray with other Christians), likewise an increasing community of worship, particularly in the service of the word (there was a most impressive service of this sort, in which Paul VI and the non-Catholic observers took part, before the close of the Council). Finally, discussions of theologians meeting as equals. The participation of non-Catholic observers at the Council today is regarded as just as obvious as the participation of Catholic observers in the various bodies of the World Council of Churches.

In order to appreciate the importance of these hastily collected, very palpable and fundamental results, we might raise the question: What would have happened in the past four hundred years of Church history if in its own day the Council of Trent—and this in itself would have been possible—had made these epoch-making decisions? But the present is more important; for the Catholic Church too the ecumenical age has irrevocably begun with Vatican II.

In this connection, what the Council decree says of the Eastern Churches in union with Rome—which have often been regarded merely as appendages of the Latin Church—will be important for the further development of ecumenism in Protestant circles also. The Churches of the East enjoy equal rights with those of the West. They have the right and duty to maintain their autonomous liturgy and legal system (the bishops nominate the patriarchs), spirituality and theology. Diversity does not injure the unity of the Church but strengthens it. In relations with the Orthodox Churches, not united with Rome, these rules hold: rebaptism of Orthodox Christians who become Catholic is not required; neither is reordination of Orthodox priests. Orthodox Christians, if they wish, may receive the sacraments in the Catholic Church; conversely, Catholic

Christians may do so in Orthodox Churches if no Catholic priest is available. Mixed marriages between Catholics and Orthodox are valid, even if they are not celebrated in the Catholic Church. Common use of churches is permitted.

But is there a clearer sign of the beginning of a new Christian age than the solemn revocation—simultaneously in Rome and in Constantinople, immediately before the close of the Council—of the mutual excommunication which in 1054 initiated almost a thousand years of schism between the Eastern and Western Churches? This bold action, asking to be followed up, shows more than many another the genuine desire of Paul VI for reconciliation. What was begun with the kiss of peace between Paul VI and the Patriarch of Constantinople in 1964 in Jerusalem found here a continuation whose positive results for the whole of Christendom cannot yet be appreciated.

B. THE CONCERNS OF THE REFORMERS

What in particular has the Council achieved in regard to Protestant Christians? Here too the Council has epoch-making results to show; it has taken up a whole series of central concerns of the Reformation. The following examples may be mentioned.

1. Esteem for the Bible. (a) In worship: this must be wholly impregnated with the biblical spirit. Psalm-singing in the mother tongue is required and in particular scriptural preaching; in every Sunday Mass there must be a sermon in which the exposition of Scripture (homily) has priority. A new, more varied cycle of Scripture readings for several years (new arrangement of pericopes) is already being prepared. (b) In the whole life of the Church. Instead of insisting on the Latin Vulgate translation (as at Trent), the demand now is for modern translations of the Bible from the original languages, produced for common use together with non-Catholics. Instead of the former prohibitions of Bible-reading by the laity (maintained into the nineteenth century), repeated invitations on every occasion to clergy and laity to read the Bible frequently. The importance of the Bible for catechetics and devo-

tion is emphasized. (c) In theology. The magisterium is not above the word of God but has to serve it. It is not the universal teaching of the Church that revealed truth is contained partly in Scripture, partly in Tradition. Biblical studies are encouraged; the study of Scripture must be the soul of theology. As opposed to all conservative attacks (cf. the dispute about the Pontifical Biblical Institute), the justification of a genuine historical-critical exposition of Scripture (literary forms, form-criticism, etc.) is expressly acknowledged. The inerrancy of Scripture is not claimed for profane statements (about natural science or history), but only for truths of salvation.

2. Genuine people's worship. In this respect, the realization of the concerns of the Reformation can be seen in a number of examples. (a) As opposed to the former clerical liturgy, the Mass offered by the whole priestly people; community emphasized through an intelligible outward form, active participation of the whole congregation in common prayer, singing and partaking of the Lord's body; private Masses thrust into the background (concelebration of several priests possible), common celebration to be preferred in principle. (b) As opposed to the former proclamation in a dead language (Latin), a new listening to the word of God intelligibly proclaimed (cf. 1 a). (c) As opposed to the former, wholly Romanized liturgy, adaptation to different nations; national episcopates to share competence to organize the liturgy instead of the former, exclusively papal competence. (d) As opposed to the former overgrowth and covering up, simplification and concentration on the essentials; revision of all the rites and thus greater resemblance of the Mass to Jesus' Last Supper. (e) Likewise, reform of the sacramental liturgy (especially revision of the rite of baptism), of the Church's year (merger of the feasts of the saints), of the priest's prayer (shorter office, in the mother tongue). (f) In this is comprised the positive settlement of classic points of controversy, about which there was often as much dispute as on questions of faith: the mother tongue at Mass and the chalice for the laity, which is likewise permitted in principle.

3. Upgrading of the laity. Direct access of the laity to Scrip-

ture and the realization of a people's worship already imply an important fulfilment of this third concern of the Reformation. In addition, however, there are the numerous theological discussions of the significance of the layman in the Church, which permeate the conciliar documents, and the implicit criticism of clericalism which is involved in this. In this connection, the Constitution on the Church is of greater importance than the decree on the lay apostolate. The Church is essentially the people of God. The laity form the universal priesthood of believers, who all share in Christ's royal, priestly and prophetic office. The charisms of the Spirit, just like the vocation to holiness, are given not only to individuals but to all. In regard to practical organization, each bishop is to form a pastoral council from priests and laymen. In the decree on the priestly ministry importance is attached to giving more respect to the laity in the life of the parish: delegating tasks, assurance of freedom of action, invitation to initiative.

4. Adaptation of the Church to the nations. As opposed to a centralized system, the importance of the local Church and particular Churches (dioceses, nations) is constantly emphasized. The national or continental bishops' conferences are to promote practical decentralization: wherever they are not yet established, they are to be juridically constituted and to meet regularly. Adaptation has already taken place, first of all, in the liturgy. But in other fields too (priests' seminaries, missions) it ought to come into effect. The resolution of the French bishops' conference to permit the worker-priests again, the resolutions of the Dutch bishops' conference, show admirably how the national episcopates can exercise their own authority. The Roman Curia itself is to be internationalized.

5. Reform of popular piety. The answers of the bishops' conferences on the question of indulgences show that the medieval system of indulgences, with which the dawn of the Lutheran Reformation was closely connected, has in fact come to an end. The reform of fasting regulations, which often concealed the specifically Christian element (Friday), has already been carried out in most countries. Finally, the dangers of a degenerating Marianism remote from Scripture and Christocentrism could be largely recog-

nized. On all this, particularly by rejecting a special Marian schema and by taking this up into the schema on the Church, Vatican II has imposed a clear limit, which has already had far-reaching consequences in practice. In spite of the wishes of some, no further Marian dogmas were defined.

If we survey this field of questions, we know that there is much that is provisional, imperfect and questionable, that quite important things are missing. Nevertheless, the question may be permitted: what in fact would Martin Luther do if he had been born in this Catholic Church of today? The answer "He would have been a *peritus* at the Council" is not entirely lacking in seriousness: many of his just demands have been largely fulfilled through this Council. But a further question may be added: Is it not the turn of the Protestant Churches effectively to approach us with a little more self-critical understanding and with a reformation of the Reformation— in the spirit of *ecclesia semper reformanda?*

C. THE TRUTH OF THE WORLD-RELIGIONS

What has the Council achieved in regard to the world-religions and particularly in regard to the Jews? There is scarcely any group of human beings to which Christendom (and certainly not only the Catholic Church) owes reparation so much as to the Jews. The enormity of National Socialist antisemitism would have been impossible without the partly covert, but often very open, "Christian" antisemitism of more than fifteen hundred years' standing, which came to light again even in the Council debates themselves.

The Council—here too John XXIII gave a personal impetus— attempts to place the relation of the Catholic Church to the Jews on a new, positive basis. She acknowledges her indissoluble bond with Israel. She too invokes the Fathers of Israel and the Scriptures. It is from Israel that Jesus and the early Church emerged. Even though the greater part of the Jews rejected Jesus as Messiah, they are not an accursed, but still the chosen, people. The responsibility for Jesus' death can be imposed neither on all the Jews of that time nor—still less—on all Jews of today. Preaching and catechetics, studies and conversations, must be made to assist mutual knowledge and esteem. The Church deplores all the phenomena of antisemitism, hatred and persecutions. She rejects any discrimination on account of race, color, class or religion.

The two or three words which were not adopted in the text are not decisive for the future. The Catholic Church has expressed herself unambiguously against any antisemitism and for co-operation with the Jews, and thus after two thousand years of Church history has introduced a new period of Christian-Jewish common life. If this turning point is to be properly evaluated, the declaration of Vatican II in 1965 should be compared—for instance—with the antisemitic measures of the most brilliant council of the Middle Ages almost exactly 750 years ago (IV Lateran, 1215).

Moreover, Vatican II has tried to improve and clarify for a new age, in a world which has become one world, relations with the world-religions, which have often been very strained, particularly in the missionary countries. The same declaration on the non-Christian religions states that all peoples with their diverse religions form a community and that in different ways these religions are attempting to answer the same vital questions. Although the Church sees the fullness of truth in Christ and his message, she does not on that account reject anything which is true and holy in other religions: rays of the one truth that enlightens all men. In conversation and co-operation, Christians are to recognize and promote the intellectual, moral and cultural values of the other religions. The Church looks with respect on Hinduism and Buddhism and especially on Islam, which with her adores the one God and honors Jesus as prophet. The centuries-old hostility between Christians and Islam must give way to understanding and a common effort for social justice, peace and freedom.

The declaration closes with a confession that all men are brothers under the one Father. It is—and this already leads to the next set of questions—striking and very significant for the relation of the Church to the modern world that the three words (so often regarded with horror) associated with the program of the French Revolution play a special role in the council texts: liberty, equality, fraternity.

D. THE SECULAR WORLD

Quite unlike—for instance—Vatican I, Vatican II reckons with the world as it really is: a world come of age. Vatican II has finally broken with the aftermath of the medieval world-view, which persisted in the Church into the nineteenth and twentieth centuries.

1. The relation of the Church to the world is dealt with in principle in the Pastoral Constitution on the Church in the Modern World. The attitude of the Church to the progress of mankind is essentially positive, though obviously not uncritical. The Church wants to be solidly united with the rest of mankind and to work together with it. Everywhere recognizing the signs of the times and interpreting them in the light of the gospel, not rejecting but answering the questions, she wants dialogue instead of polemics, convincing testimony instead of conquest. Precisely in virtue of her own message she wants to stand up resolutely for the dignity, freedom and rights of man, for the development and improvement of the human community and its institutions, for the healthy dynamism of all human creation.

2. The same constitution gives concrete expression to the positive attitude of the Church, particularly in the following points: (a) an attitude of understanding and self-criticism towards the different forms of atheism (communism is not mentioned, in order to avoid political misunderstandings); (b) emphasis on mutual love and human responsibility in married life; (c) the affirmation of responsible freedom in intellectual and cultural creativity, of the justified autonomy of the sciences and of theological study related to life; (d) a special stand on behalf of the weak (peoples and individuals) in economic, social and political life; (e) a sharp rejection of war and especially atomic war (the passage on the dangers of possessing atomic weapons was opposed only by a small, non-representative group of the North-American episco-

pate, and this was in vain) and co-operation in building up an international community of peoples (the very impressive gesture of reconciliation on the part of the Polish and German episcopate at the end of the Council provides an example of this).

3. Finally, the Declaration on Religious Freedom—in spite of changes for the worse in the text, which likewise emerged only in the final editing—belongs to the great future-pointing documents of the Council. It states: (a) Every human being has the right to freedom of religion. It pertains to the dignity of the human person to be able to act—particularly in religious matters—according to his conscience, free from any coercion, privately and publicly, as an individual and in community. (b) Every religious community has the right to unhampered public practice of religion in accordance with its own laws. It should be free in regard to its worship, the selection, training and appointment of its pastors, dealing with Church leaders and the other communities throughout the world, the erection of buildings for worship and the ownership of material possessions, public testimony to its faith in speech and writing (unless dishonorable means are used), participation in the building up of social life. (c) Freedom of religion must be protected and promoted by society, state and Church. Where, as a result of historical development, a particular religious community enjoys a special position at law, the right of all citizens and religious communities to freedom of religion must at the same time be granted and protected. The fact that the free exercise of religion is also limited by the rights of others and the common good must not lead the state to act arbitrarily or in a partisan spirit against a particular community. In human society the principle holds good: as much freedom as possible, as much restriction as necessary. If the Church today takes up a position on religious freedom different from that of former times, she does so because she is following Christ's gospel.

It can certainly be expected that this last declaration particularly will have an influence on the position of Protestants in Catholic countries (and perhaps also in abolishing anti-Catholic articles of the constitution in countries like Switzerland).

E. REFORM OF THE CHURCH

What has the Catholic Church done about her own reform? All that has been said up to now might be repeated here. What the Council has done in relation to other Christians (especially in realizing the concerns of the Orthodox and of the Reformers) and in relation to the world and its religions is the result of an inward change, of a renewal which has seized the Church herself. But we are not going to talk again here about the liturgical, biblical, ecumenical, pastoral renewal in which the demands for reform raised for decades or centuries have been fulfilled (at least partially). Only new features in theological self-understanding and Church structure will be summarily indicated.

1. A new ecclesial self-understanding: the clerical, legalistic and triumphalist conception of the Church of the Middle Ages and the Counter-Reformation begins in the constitution to undergo a decisive alteration. Here the Church is no longer understood simply as a supernatural authoritarian state, with the Pope as absolute monarch at the head, then the aristocracy of bishops and priests, and finally the faithful in a passive role—as the people in the sense of "subjects." The constitution is no longer identified with the hierarchy. The Church is seen more from within: as a "mystery," announced in the diverse metaphors of the Bible, not to be confused with political organisms. At the same time, the conception of the Church as the people of God is fundamental: the people of God constantly on the way through history, a pilgrim people in sinfulness and in a provisional, eschatological situation, constantly ready for fresh reforms. The whole Church exists in the local Churches. The office-holders are not above but in the people of God. They are no more and no less than servants of the people, which indeed as a whole is priestly and equipped with the gifts of the Spirit.

2. Pope and bishops: the Pope is not an absolute monarch. Without prejudice to his primacy, it is expressly laid down in the Constitution on the Church that the bishops together with the Pope

have a communal responsibility for the whole Church. This holds true not only for an ecumenical council but permanently. The expression and organ of this collegiality in future is to be the episcopal council (the synod of bishops) which was established by the Pope at the beginning of the fourth session, at the wish of the Council: as distinct from the college of cardinals, it was to be proportionally (!) composed, predominantly from the chosen (!) representatives of the bishops' conferences. These bishops' conferences form an essential factor in decentralization. They are to meet regularly and can occasionally make decisions binding on all bishops. They are to divide dioceses afresh, so that these are not too large and not too small (episcopal sees in more suitable places); likewise, new ecclesiastical provinces and ecclesiastical regions are to be created. Bishops have ordinary, autonomous and immediate authority over their dioceses. In future they can dispense from the universal law of the Church in individual cases, unless the contrary is expressly laid down.

3. The Roman Curia. This is to be reformed in accordance with the requirements of the present time and of the different nations, in regard to spheres of competence, manner of procedure and coordination. It is to be at the service of the bishops. Above all, it is to be internationalized (inclusion of diocesan bishops and consultation of laymen). The competence of papal nuncios and delegates in relation to bishops is to be more precisely defined. Before the close of the Council, Paul VI once again confirmed the will to reform so clearly manifested in the address to the Curia before the second session.

The reform of the office of the Roman Inquisition, of the Holy Office, marks the beginning of Paul VI's reform of the Curia. This office, now called "The Congregation for the Doctrine of Faith," loses its priority as the supreme congregation. In its procedures it is subject to universal canon law (publication of the order of procedure, hitherto kept secret). There can no longer be any condemnation without the accused being given an opportunity to defend himself and his own bishop being given a hearing. The office has to be open-minded in regard to modern scholarship: close relations with the Biblical Commission, consultation of experts, organization of study conferences. It must be acknowledged that some things have already improved in the work of this office, which was severely criticized at the Council. The Index of Prohibited Books—as Cardinal Ottaviani announced—has died a natural death. In some cases, where the office had made a mistake, the decisions were expressly withdrawn.

4. Priests and priestly training. (a) The particular priestly task within the universal priesthood of all is the special ministry of preaching the word, administering the sacraments, leading the congregation. The priest must not be separated from the people, but united fraternally with men in the midst of the world. Wholly human, he is to witness to the gospel by his whole existence. Between bishop and priests a friendly relationship of mutual consultation and co-operation should exist. In every diocese a senate of priests is to be formed, representing the "presbyterium" of the diocese and effectively supporting the bishop in ruling the diocese. Priesthood and manual labor are to be reconciled with one another. Priests in the Eastern Churches united with Rome, who even today are married in accordance with the old tradition, are no less priests than those in the West. Even in the Latin Church, fathers of families are envisaged for the office of deacons which is to be re-established.

(b) The Council deliberately avoids giving detailed regulations for priestly training. For seminaries in their countries the bishops' conferences are to set up their own scheme, which is to be revised at definite intervals and approved by the Pope. In this way priestly training should always be adapted to the particular circumstances of time and place. For spirituality the predominant factor must be the gospel rather than particular, traditional forms of piety. Study of the Bible in particular is to be promoted as the soul of all theology. Dogmatics, too, should start out from biblical themes and from these proceed by way of history of dogma and theology to systematic penetration. Teaching methods are to be tested, outdated questions no longer discussed. Receptivity to the world is to be promoted in every way: knowledge too of contemporary philosophy and of the progress of the natural sciences; awareness of the characteristic developments of the present time; cultivation of genuine and opportune human values; preparation for conversation with men of today and ability to listen; knowledge of the Christian Churches and religions in the country concerned; practical-pastoral training. The order of the house is to be adapted to the age of the students, to train them in greater independence and the intelligent use of freedom.

(c) The individual religious communities (their general chapters) have themselves to undertake a radical renewal and to provide also the possibility of experimenting. Return to the origins (the primary thing is the gospel, not the rule of the order) and adaptation to changed temporal circumstances are the criteria by which all constitutions, regulations and customs are to be tested, obsolete provisions eliminated, but at the same time without increasing the number of regulations. Institutes and monasteries which show no promise of any fruitful activity may no longer accept novices and are to join up as far as possible with healthier communities.

5. Missions. The Church's missionary mandate is justified theologically, even though the unbaptized person is not excluded from salvation. The young Churches must draw whatever they can from the customs, traditions, doctrines, arts and social systems of their peoples. In view of this task, theological study should be directed afresh to the biblical revelation; the mode of thought of these peoples must be kept in mind in theology. The communities of Christians are to remain culturally and socially rooted in the people as a whole and, above all, bear witness to an all-embracing love. There should be dialogue and co-operation, but no interference of the Church in state business. The missions particularly are to help in overcoming the scandal of the divisions of Christendom, which are especially perceptible in missionary countries: as far as possible, there should be common witness and co-operation of the Churches. The Roman Congregation is to look for ways and means of co-ordinating missionary work with the other Christian missions. The council of bishops is to give special attention to missionary activity. The supreme direction of missionary activity as a whole is

to have a body, which will assemble periodically, composed of representatives of the missionary Churches and the leaders of the pontifical missionary aid societies (thus responsibility no longer belongs solely to the Roman Congregation for the missions).

The comprehensive program of Vatican II for internal reform of the Church will mean a great deal of work in the coming years. But at the same time there are things which must not be forgotten, although they are not formulated in the decrees and will perhaps be of even great significance for the next decades:

1. A new spirit, going beyond all the formulations, has become alive in the Catholic Church.

2. A new freedom of thinking and discussion has proved supremely fruitful.

3. A new, more historical-existential relationship to truth has become a reality.

4. The fragmentary character and historical contingency of all the documents of the Church's teaching was concretely experienced.

5. The "infallibility" defined at Vatican I was deliberately not invoked by Vatican II.

6. The neo-scholastic textbook theology has betrayed its incapacity for solving the new problems.

7. The authority of a living theology and of theologians altogether has been decisively strengthened.

8. A new ideal of Church government has become visible at all levels (instead of one-man government, common responsibility).

9. The Church has abandoned the specifically medieval basic attitude, especially in regard to society, state, politics, scholasticism.

10. The just concerns of the Eastern Churches and of the Reformation have been admitted in the Catholic Church.

At the close of the Council, I often recalled the suggestions in my book *The Council, Reform and Reunion,* which appeared before the Council. These demands were then regarded as the maximum possible; many considered them extremist. With regard to the suggestions then made, I may today say that the Council has not indeed done everything which—from the standpoint of the present situation—it might have done, but it has done far more than was ever expected of it before it opened. At that time I wrote: "The Council will be either the fulfilment of a great hope or else a great disappointment. The fulfilment of a *small* hope would—given the grave world situation and the needs of Christendom—be in fact a great disappointment" (p. 148). Today I may say that in spite of all the disappointments, which are by no means slight, the Council has brought about the fulfilment of a great hope. It forms a solid, even though not unproblematic, basis for the way of the post-conciliar Church into the future.

VII/Change of Course in Doctrine?

EVERY NEW historical situation carries with it new difficulties and dangers. The Catholic Church too will have to reckon with new difficulties and dangers on her way into a new and, by and large, only sketchily perceptible future. It is no more than normal if the spectacular change of course has not only relieved us of many, very many cares, but has also imposed some new ones on us. Tensions, which often are not slight, bearing witness to new life, have dissolved the former conformist, graveyard peace. On the whole, the Catholic Church has surmounted this reorientation remarkably well: scarcely any similar occurrence of this magnitude—something like an "orderly revolution"—can be observed in Church history. And this is not merely a fine program announced by some lofty ecclesiastical body without authority, as is sometimes the case with the decisions of the World Council of Churches, but a renewal with very incisive theological and also practical consequences, which extend deeply into the concrete life of the individual parish throughout the world. It has happened too—by contrast to Vatican I with its new dogmas—without splitting off a part of the Church. What other Church would have been able to achieve anything like what Vatican II achieved?

Hence we shall come to terms also with the new problems. We have suffered under an authoritatively prescribed problem bottleneck, and the pressure resulting from this, for so long that a lowering of defenses is bound to lead to some turbulence, to whirlpools and rapids. And, accustomed as we have been to still waters, it will at first not be wholly easy to swim in the rapid stream of an often incalculable history. Fossilization in a "Catholicism" which is in fact no longer post-Tridentine, but post-Vatican—feared by some during the time of the Council—is scarcely a danger to be taken seriously at present, if the church is not judged merely by the often smooth, official surface. The post-conciliar agitation is significantly greater than expected precisely in the deeper strata of church people and especially among the intellectuals and in theology.

In such a situation it has certainly not been made easy for those in the Church who exercise a ministry, for the pastoral ministries; and it is not surprising that some bishops and parish priests groan under the new, unexpected demands. In fact, there is scarcely anything still to be gained from the purely external authority of a particular office or title. Only genuine, intrinsic authority will be able to prevail, an authority therefore which is based on human qualities, on technical competence, and on co-operation in a spirit of partnership. This genuine authority must prevail, especially in the post-conciliar Church, and it must be able to establish itself in the right way: a tumultuous and chaotic development would in fact do serious damage, not only to the Catholic Church but also, indirectly, to all other Christian Churches and the whole of Christendom.

Naturally, special difficulties are created by the change of course in Catholic *teaching;* in a certain sense this is a test-case for ecclesial truthfulness. We should apply ourselves fearlessly and in complete sincerity to these uncertainties. Inside the Catholic Church, and outside it to some extent, people have taken a poor view of Vatican II's attempt to suppress the fact of the change of course in doctrine —or at any rate, its failure to express the change clearly: as if both the Catholic Church and the popes had "always" taught what they are teaching today on controversial points. Actually it may be impossible to assert, still more so to prove theologically, a continuity in all the points of recent Catholic teaching. The Church's path over the last hundred years is not a dead-straight throughway. How could it have been, in the chaos and confusion of our times?

We can see at once how all contradictions could be explained away as a consistent development only by using the methods of totalitarian party ideologists ("for the party is always right"), if we simply compare the authoritative doctrinal document from the sixties of the last century, just before Vatican I—Pius IX's "Syllabus or Summary of the Main Errors of Our Age" (1864)—with the doctrinal documents of Vatican II. The development theory reaches its limit at the point where the opposite is expressly asserted.

The *affirmation* of modern progress, of modern liberal achievements and of modern civilization, by the Pastoral Constitution on the Church in the Modern World (1965), cannot possibly be understood as "development" of that teaching of 1864 in which the proposition was solemnly *condemned*: "The Roman Pontiff can and should reconcile and harmonize himself with progress, with Liberalism, and with modern civilization" (DS 2980). The pair of opposites—explicit and implicit—usually invoked in the theory of development of dogma also breaks down here. The *affirmation* of freedom of religion at Vatican II is contained neither explicitly nor implicitly in the *condemnation* of freedom of religion by Pius IX. Nor can the question be avoided by saying that times have altered so much and that the intention then was to condemn only the negative excesses of freedom of religion (and of similar modern achievements). It is sufficient to read the condemnations themselves. Error 77: "In our time it is no longer expedient to recognize the Catholic religion as the sole religion of the state, to the exclusion of any other forms of worship" (DS 2977). Error 78: "Hence it is laudable in certain Catholic countries to provide by law for the people immigrating thither to be allowed publicly to practise their own religion, of whatever form it may be" (DS 2978). Error 79: "For it is false that civil liberty for any kind of cult and likewise the full power granted to all of proclaiming openly and publicly any kind of opinions and ideas easily leads to corruption of the minds and morals of nations and to the propagation of the plague of indifferentism" (DS 2979).

Much the same could be said—although perhaps less verbatim —of other condemned propositions: for instance, in regard to impeding the free progress of science by Roman decrees (DS 2912; cf. now Pope Paul VI's stipulations for reform of the Inquisition and the Holy Office); in regard to the dubious adaptability of scholastic methods and principles in theology to the needs of the time (DS 2913; cf. now the demand in the decrees on priestly formation and ecumenism, for theological methods starting out from Scripture); in regard to the questioning of the Church's claim to temporal power and of the necessity of a large ecclesiastical state (DS 2924, 2927, 2934, 2955, 2975, 2976; cf. now the general presentation of the Church in all the documents of Vatican II as a spiritual factor, which is in the world not to rule but to serve); in regard to the rejection of a share of the popes in the guilt of the Eastern schism (DS 2938; cf. now the admissions of guilt of both Pope and Council in regard to the schism of the Eastern and Western Church); in regard to the condemnation of any good hope for the eternal salvation of all those who are not living in the true Church of Christ (DS 2917; cf. now the explicit affirmation in the Constitution on the Church of the possibility of salvation for all men even outside the Church, even for convinced, sincere atheists), and so on.

But why should we, particularly as Christians—why should the Catholic Church particularly, which takes her stand on the *gospel of Jesus Christ*—be ashamed of having learned something more in the last hundred years, of having been changed for the better, of having finally done what far-seeing Catholic theologians and laymen had also already demanded at that time? Why should we be ashamed of being capable of *metanoia,* of change of mind and heart, as a Church of human beings under God's grace and, through the guidance of the Holy Spirit, capable of a real turning away from former ignorance, inexperience and incapacity, limitation and superficiality; from former diversions, side tracks, wrong tracks; from misunderstandings, mistakes and errors; capable of a real turning towards better knowledge, insight, clear sight, lucidity; to greater certainty, rectitude, closeness to life, reality; to greater truth? *Conversio,* then, to *veritas semper major,* to the ever greater truth, behind which is hidden no other than *Deus semper major,* the ever greater God.

Today—very differently from former times—we do not take it badly if anyone says that he has changed his opinion, that he has revised, corrected his view, that today he would see it differently, better, or in the opposite way. We respect a person for saying this. We take it badly only if someone changes his mind but does not admit it; when a person says the opposite of what he said before, but now asserts that he had always said it. For modern man it is not the revision of a position but the negations of a revision which offend against truthfulness. And so people respect a Church too which today tries to do better, which has positively changed her mind about many things, which today wants to live more with men in the modern world, wants to understand them better, which thus not only preaches *metanoia,* conversion, to others but practises it herself.

There is no doubt that the Church as a whole has gained greatly in credibility in the world through the new, conciliar orientation. At the same time, unfortunately, the fact must be accepted that some who kept loyally to the former regulations (in regard to fasting laws, Latin and liturgy, especially) now feel that they are disowned. If in regard to a particular question the Church has brought very much suffering on human beings, through a false or at least out-of-date approach, then precisely those affected ought to understand that she must change her attitude in order not to create still more suffering (this holds analogously too for the law of celibacy). It would hardly be Christian to say: "We had to suffer, the others must suffer too."

Certainly bishops and teachers in the Church ought to grasp fully all possibilities, and better than hitherto, in order to explain and render intelligible why the Church then spoke in one way and today speaks differently. There are actually always very many factors involved in Church and society at a particular time, which make people behave then in one way and not in another. And it is always possible to give many reasons why today we have struggled through to a different outlook. But this justification must not be made a cheap excuse, a tacit dispensation, from accepting unhesitatingly full responsibility also for the human failure of the Church and her government. What will be decisive is to learn from all the failures and do things better in the future—and this means now, at the present time. Just so ought the church constantly to seek afresh to win the trust of men.

But is there not very much more at stake here? More than confidence in the Church? Have we not hitherto overlooked the decisive perspective, that confidence on which all confidence in the Church is based: confidence in the Holy Spirit? A difficult problem-complex emerges here, and it can be fully understood why—for example—particularly in the question of birth control, the conservative minority of the Roman commission which the Pope backed wanted this point treated with the utmost seriousness.

It had in fact been clear for a long time before Pope Paul VI's encyclical that the real dispute is not about the pill, not about birth regulation at all, but about the truth of the Church's magisterium. It had become more and more established, even in the Catholic Church, that the teaching on birth control ought to be changed; but could it be admitted that the magisterium of the Catholic Church had made a mistake? We shall try to find our way towards answering this question, raised by so many. On this point, too, only complete truthfulness can get us out of the present crisis.

1. The conservative theology of the minority on the commission is right in insisting that the problem must not be simplified by saying that the encyclical of Pius XI, *Casti Connubii,* of 1930, was not an *"infallible"* statement. It can in fact be shown with overwhelming documentation from statements of the popes, of the bishops' conferences, and of so many outstanding individual bishops and of the universal teaching of theologians, that, at least in our century, it is a question of a universal teaching, binding under grave sin, of the Church's magisterium *(magisterium ordinarium).*

A doctrine taught so intensively and universally is equivalent to an "infallible" doctrinal statement. Thus the conservative group rightly argues:

> Our question is a question of the *truth* of this proposition: contraception is always seriously evil. The truth of this teaching stems from the fact that it has been proposed with such constancy, with such universality, with such obligatory force, always and everywhere, as something to be held and followed by the faithful. Technical and juridical investigation into the irreformability and infallibility of *Casti Connubii* (as if once this obstacle had been removed, the true doctrine could be found and taught) distracts from the central question and even prejudices the question.[1]

2. Conservative theology is again right in saying that a change in teaching cannot be explained simply by a different historical situation. For already in 1930 the Lambeth Conference of the Anglican bishops had presented precisely the solution and the reasons for birth control which are offered to support it today:

> For, as a matter of fact, the teaching of *Casti Connubii* was solemnly proposed in opposition to the doctrine of the Lambeth Conference of 1930, by the Church "to whom God has entrusted the defense of the integrity and purity of morals . . . in token of her divine ambassadorship . . . and through our mouth." . . . Some who fight for a change say that the teaching of the Church was not false for those times. Now, however, it must be changed because of changed historical conditions. But this seems to be something that one cannot propose, for the Anglican Church was teaching precisely that and for the very reasons which the Catholic Church solemnly denied, but which it would now admit. Certainly such a manner of speaking would be unintelligible to the people and would seem to be a specious pretext.[2]

3. Conservative theology is again right in saying that we would have to admit honestly that the Church's magisterium has seriously and quite formally erred:

> If contraception were declared not intrinsically evil, in honesty it would have to be acknowledged that the Holy Spirit in 1930 (Encycli-

cal, *Casti Connubii*), 1951 (Address of Pius XII to midwives) and 1958 (Address to the International Congress of Haematologists in the year of Pius XII's death), assisted Protestant Churches, and that for half a century Pius XI, Pius XII and a great part of the Catholic hierarchy did not protest against a very serious error, one most pernicious to souls; for it would thus be suggested that they condemned most imprudently, under pain of eternal punishment, thousands upon thousands of human acts which are now approved. Indeed, it must be neither denied nor ignored that these acts would be approved for the same fundamental reasons which Protestantism alleged and which they (Catholics) condemned or at least did not recognize.[3]

4. Conservative theology is *not* right only in *doubting the assistance of the Holy Spirit* in the event of having to admit such errors. But here precisely is its real argument against a change in the teaching on birth control, in which the whole line of proof culminates:

> What is more, however, this change would inflict a grave blow on the teaching about the assistance of the Holy Spirit, promised to the Church to lead the faithful on the right way toward their salvation. . . . For the Church to have erred so gravely in its grave responsibility of leading souls would be tantamount to seriously suggesting that the assistance of the Holy Spirit was lacking to her.[4]

The trust of Christians in God's Spirit in the Church must be very much stronger. And, thanks be to God, it has already in fact always been stronger. For it would be thoroughly naive to assume that an error in the question of birth control is the first serious error that has crept into the Church's magisterium.

This book would become very thick if we were to try to give an account of all that could be noted on the negative side. We may recall the excommunication of the Patriarch Photius and of the Greek Church, which rendered formal the now nearly thousand-year-old schism with the Eastern Church; the prohibition of interest, another extremely pressing moral question on which the Church's magisterium changed its views far too late; the condemnation of Galileo, which is essentially responsible for the alienation between the Church and the natural sciences; the condemnation of new forms of worship in the rites controversy, which is a main reason for the far-reaching breakdown of the Catholic missions of modern times in India, China and Japan; the maintenance of the Pope's medieval secular power even into modern times, with all the secular and spiritual means of excommunication, which rendered the papacy further incredible as a spiritual ministry; the numerous condemnations of modern historical-critical exegesis (in regard to the authorship of the books of the Bible, source-criticism, historicity and literary forms, the Johannine Comma, the Vulgate); or the condemnations in the dogmatic field, particularly in connection with "Modernism" (theory of evolution, conception of the development of dogma) and so on.

Everywhere here reasonable and courageous theologians, priests and laypeople, even then—at the time when these wrong decisions were reached—had rightly seen and mostly also warned against them; but they could not prevail against the theological party which made use of the central lever of curial power (Holy office, papal diplomacy, Congregation for the Propagation of the Faith, Biblical Commission).

Everywhere here, then, the magisterium, which in fact is represented by sinful and erring human beings, has erred. Everywhere here the magisterium—mostly of course "implicitly," discreetly—has corrected itself. Even the conservative minority on the commission today frankly admits such errors, but minimizes them, by making innocuous the truly catastrophic decisions and asserting that it was a "question of peripheral matters (as, for example, the case of Galileo), or of an excess in the way a thing is done (the excommunication of Photius)." [5]

It was very much to the credit of Pope Paul VI, with his great solicitude for the relations of the Catholic Church to the Orthodox Churches and to modern science, that in any case he took these questions much more seriously and that he deliberately honored in public the name of Galileo, on which previous popes were silent, and has publicly withdrawn the excommunication against the Patriarch of Constantinople. And it is also very much to the credit of the theologians who made available the moral theological expert opinion

for the progressive majority of the commission, that they spoke
with unusual frankness about the errors of the Church's magisterium, not least in regard to marital morality:

> Not a few theologians and faithful fear that a change in the official
> teaching could damage the confidence of Catholics in the teaching
> authority of the Church. For they ask how the assistance of the Holy
> Spirit could permit such an error for so many centuries, and one that
> has had so many consequences, especially in recent centuries. But
> the criteria for discerning what the Spirit could or could not permit
> in the Church can scarcely be determined *a priori*. In point of fact, we
> know that there have been errors in the teaching of the magisterium
> and of tradition. With regard to intercourse one should note that for
> so many centuries in the Church, with the active concurrence of the
> Popes, it was all but unanimously taught that marital intercourse was
> illicit unless accompanied by the intention to procreate—or at least
> (because of the words of I Cor. 7) to offer an outlet for the other
> partner; and yet no theologians hold to this teaching today, nor is it
> the official position.[6]

Certainly the conclusion could not have been avoided that a new,
critical interpretation of the Church's "infallibility" could overcome
the present difficulties.

No: the confidence of Christians and also of theologians in God's
Spirit in the Church must be very much stronger. And this not only
in fact, in the concrete endurance of the errors of the magisterium
in the past and present, but also as a matter of theological principle.

Or ought we perhaps to believe in God's providence in the
world only insofar as nothing serious befalls us? May we ever begin to doubt this providence when international catastrophes shake
the world or even particular blows of fate shatter our life? Can we
believe in God's providence in the world only when we can be
certain, at least in particular cases, at least in particular fields, at
least with particular, important persons, that God's providence
permits no misfortune, no catastrophe, no sin and no error? All
this would be perhaps a reassuring thought, wanting to exclude
any risk, but it is certainly not the venture of a serious faith in
God's providence. It would be rather a part of the fainthearted-

ness of the disciples of Jesus at all times, whom every storm on the journey throws into fear and doubt and who think they have to wake the Lord, because they are perishing, then only to be told: "Why are you afraid, O men of little faith?" (Mt. 8:26).

As long as everything goes well in the world, it is easy to believe in a divine providence in the world; this the optimistic men of the "Enlightenment" did too, until the great earthquake of Lisbon with its 30,000 dead. As long as nothing important goes wrong with the Church, it is easy to believe in the special assistance of the Holy Spirit in the Church. Yet belief in God's providence in the world is proved precisely in the face of evil, wickedness, sin, error in the Church—and in this connection we must not forget that sin is essentially worse than all error, which is in fact not sinful, but merely human.

A person who does not take his faith here as radically serious, who is fainthearted and afraid, in the last resort does not take seriously precisely the fundamental *infallibility* of the Church—and the infallibility of the pope according to Vatican I (DS 3074) is no other than that of the Church, although Vatican I did not reflect on the infallibility of the Church as such. In-fallibility of the Church means: insofar as the Church is humbly obedient to God's word and will, she shares in the truth of Spirit of God in the Church (*Deus revelans*), who can neither deceive (*fallere*) nor be deceived (*falli*) (DS 3008). She is then far above lying and fraud (*omnis fallacia*) and all deception (*omne fallax*). Infallibility in this radical sense means a *basic persistence of the Church in truth, which is not destroyed by errors in detail.*

Anyone whose trust in God and in his Spirit is not superficial or rationalist, but profoundly Christian, believes unshakably that the Spirit of God will maintain the Church in the truth of the gospel, in *spite* of all errors and *through* all errors. This is the great miracle of the Holy Spirit of God in the Church: not that no errors occur —where then would be the humanity of the Church of men? —but that the Church, in spite of all her defection from God, is never dropped by God, never abandoned by God; that, in spite of all sins and errors of popes, bishops, priests, theologians and laymen, she did not perish like the dynasties of the Pharaohs and the Roman Empire of the Caesars, but continues to be sustained by God in the Spirit throughout the centuries and—even after long periods of decadence—is led to ever new life and new truth. Particularly here it is strikingly evident that the truth and truthfulness of the Church is not her own achievement, but the incomprehensible event of God's merciful grace. And our faith rejoices in the thought that ultimately our own endurance in truth although we constantly fail, is indeed important, but not ultimately decisive. What is much more decisive is the great promise of his fidelity, which God will not revoke in all eternity, in spite of our failure all along the line.

So the storm then may still rage so fiercely and darkness fall; the ship of the Church may toss and roll, it may lose its course and drift hither and thither aimlessly with sails slackened: ". . . he will give you another Counselor, to be with you for ever, even the Spirit of truth" (Jn. 14:16–17). She will not succumb to the power of darkness, of lying and fraud. She is certain: by God's gracious promise, infallibility is bestowed on her. In spite of all her erring and misunderstanding, she is maintained in truth by God.

Thus we see that the infallibility of the Church, from the standpoint of the Scriptures (and also affirmed by the Reformers) is much more than the infallibility of certain (and ultimately in fact always ambiguous, because human) ecclesial *propositions*. It is more fundamental, more comprehensive, than an *a priori* indubitably ascertainable infallibility of particular propositions. This kind of infallibility cannot be directly proved from the New Testament; it is disputed among particular Churches (not only in regard to the pope, but also in regard to the bishops and their councils) and at any rate on the basis described—with which Vatican I never really came to terms—it ought to be freshly examined. Whatever may be the outcome of the inquiry, acceptance in the concrete of errors in the Church can never mean treating light-heartedly ecclesiastical professions of faith and definitions which have the whole Church behind them. All irresponsibility here takes its revenge on the Church.

Even if we must allow in a quite radical way more than hitherto for the fragmentary character of all ecclesiastical formulations of faith—Paul in 1 Corinthians 13:9–13 uses such expressions as imperfect, unfinished, enigmatic, partial, fragmentary, as in a mirror—so indeed at the same time also—and this had already always been a justified concern of Catholic theology—we must recognize the special binding character of those formulations of faith behind which, in any sort of form, the whole Church stands. And this not only for the more extrinsic reason that, without a definition in the broadest sense, experience shows that a chaotic situation in proclamation and teaching can scarcely be avoided, but for the intrinsic reason that the formulations of faith which are a testimony of the totality of the faithful possess as testimonies a *qualitatively* higher value than the formulations of faith of an individual Christian or theologian (the distinction in a community between the individual and the whole is in fact not merely numerical-quantitative).

The result is that the individual Christian and theologian—for all the right and duty of criticism—have to be seriously concerned about agreement with a profession of faith or definition of the whole Church in quite a different way from that in which they are concerned about a profession or definition of an individual. The latter—no matter how right it may sometimes be and no matter how much it may then also perhaps come to prevail in the Church —is to be evaluated in the first place simply as the personal conviction or opinion of an individual. We shall not be forced to choose between the alternatives *either* of the fragmentary *or* the binding character of the Church's formulations of faith if in proclamation and "magisterium" a genuine counterplay and interplay exists between the authority of the whole Church and the authority of the individual, and in particular between the authority of the *pastores* (pastoral ministries) and of the *doctores* (teaching ministries.) [7]

Only in loyal, free co-operation as partners in complete truthfulness shall we be able to master constructively the new difficulties, and not least these new problems in the Church's teaching and proclamation. There is not simply *the* Church's teaching office as there is *the* foreign office. Apart from the fact that, together with the pope, the bishops too, and, together with the bishops, the parish priests too and their assistants are entrusted with the teaching, so even in textbook theology a distinction has always rightly been made between a *magisterium authenticum* and a *magisterium scientificum*.

This terminology is not, indeed, the best, inasmuch as the authenticity of the teaching is not simply assured by a particular ministerial position in the Church. But, presupposing this distinction, we might say: the "authentic" magisterium should be as authentic as possible and the "scientific" magisterium as scientific as possible. Then they will best complement one another to the advantage of the Church. In biblical terms, following Paul, it is preferable to speak of "pastoral ministries" and "teaching ministries."

Pastors cannot without more ado be teachers nor teachers without more ado pastors. The theologian in the Church takes too much on himself if in his teaching ministry he wants also to take over Church government. But conversely the pastor too assumes too much if, in addition to his pastoral ministry, he wants also to decide questions of scientific theology in an authoritarian fashion.

Pastors and teachers have their specific task in the Church, which they are to fulfil for the benefit of the communities in common responsibility towards the same gospel and in fraternal co-operation with one another. Whether the Catholic Church will emerge whole and without damage from the change of course in doctrine so obvious today will depend quite essentially on this interplay of mutual respect and mutual assistance. We have no doubt that the Church will successfully endure this test case of ecclesial truthfulness too and emerge strengthened from all the very real difficulties.

NOTES

1. Reprinted in *The Tablet,* London, April 29, 1967, pp. 480-481.
2. *Ibid.,* p. 485.
3. *Ibid.,* pp. 483-484.

4. *Ibid.*, p. 485.
5. *Ibid.*, p. 485.
6. *The Tablet*, May 6, 1967, p. 511.
7. Cf. further on the complex problems of an ecclesiastical infallibility my *Strukturen der Kirche* VIII; *Structures of the Church* (New York, Nelson, 1963): *Theologie und Kirche* (Einsiedeln, 1964); *Die Kirche* D III, 2c.; *The Church* (New York, 1968).

VIII/Manipulation of Truth?

THE CHURCH which does not conceal her mistakes, but constructively comes to terms with them, is, because truthful, also credible. A more truthful and therefore more credible Church may expect and demand more understanding, more loyalty, more commitment, particularly in regard to her teaching, her creeds, declarations and definitions. Nevertheless some questions remain.

Can, then, untruthfulness in teaching be altogether avoided if a person as a Christian, and particularly as a theologian, feels bound by certain creeds, declarations and definitions of his Church? Is a critical discussion possible at all, once binding definitions of the community are accepted? Under such circumstances, does not a manipulation of truth become inevitable, in order to maintain the doctrinal system?

By "manipulation of truth" we mean here that truth is put at the disposal of the system and politically managed. Words are used, not for communication, but for domination. Language is corrupted through tactical ambiguity, objective untruth, distorted rhetoric and shallow pathos. What is not clear can thus be made to seem clear and the clear to seem not clear. One's own position is extolled and the opponent condemned out of hand, without serious argument. If continuity is lacking, it can be procured by omissions and harmonizations. The admission and correction of errors is strictly avoided, and instead a practical omniscience of authority insinu-

141

ated. It is no longer a question of an untiring quest for truth, but of the inert, imaginary possession of truth, maintained by every instrument of power.

This manipulation of truth is rampant above all in the totalitarian systems, where the ruling party "possesses" all truth. Many reproach the Catholic Church for the same sort of thing and frequently find there too—at least in the past—the consequences of such a manipulation of truth: free discussion is suspect, dissenters are morally disqualified; within the dominant machinery of bureaucracy truth is the result of political struggle, of the power game of different pressure groups; secrecy is demanded in things that concern everyone; scholarship consequently must serve the system; people speak differently in private from what they do in public, they speak differently from what they write; through fear of commitment they take refuge in esoteric spheres of study, far from the storms, and for the rest adapt themselves tacitly to the party line. Thus people escape from the real difficulties of life, the most urgent decisions are postponed. Anxious and opportunist— but therefore not particularly scrupulous—prestige-, power-, and system-thinking is dominant, not humility and respect for truth. In these circumstances, truth is "politically" utilized, used up, abused, instead of being truthfully thought out, respected, loved, lived.

These reproaches cannot be examined in detail here. If they are generalized, then they are certainly unjust. But no one can overlook the fact that they contain much that is valid. Where there are human beings there is also misuse of truth and—as everywhere, so also in the Church and in ourselves—we have constantly to renew the struggle against it. Yet such a fundamental answer must not allow us to forget that the question of a manipulation of truth in the Church has its specific aspect—insofar, that is, as the Church's creeds, declarations and definitions present quite special problems and create special difficulties.

How are we to come to terms constructively, for instance—to name an example important not only for Catholic theology—with a doctrinal statement so steeped in tradition as "No salvation outside the Church," [1] without in any way lapsing at the same time into untruthfulness? Vatican II, for instance, has insisted that non-members of the Catholic Church too, even declared atheists, can gain salvation; but nowhere has the Council expressly corrected the axiom itself. It cannot be reproached for this, inasmuch as it reflects only the usual or even relatively progressive Catholic and partly also Protestant theology. And yet the question arises: Is not theology here manipulating truth in an untruthful fashion, when on the one hand it proclaims "no salvation outside" and on the other expressly admits "salvation outside," when in fact it teaches the opposite *in reality* but retains the *formula*? And some then ask, What is the point? to assert a continuity that does not exist? in order not to disavow a magisterium that has exceeded its authority?

It will be very important, particularly in regard to the ecclesiastical formularies of faith—whether they are creeds of the early Church, Catholic dogmas or Protestant confessions of faith—to proceed with absolute truthfulness. How this is possible, and which is the better way of achieving it, will be briefly indicated in the following distinctions.

1. A *positivistic* interpretation of professions of faith easily collides with truthfulness. The axiom "no salvation outside" in a positivistic interpretation is taken verbally and literally, as verbally and literally as a jurist interprets and applies the law. The question is not raised as to its derivation, how it has changed, whether it still means anything, how it might be better formulated. As juridical positivism rejects every principle that does not arise from positive law and regards the existing law as the beginning and end of law and justice, so dogmatic positivism takes the official ecclesiastical documents as the beginning and end of theology, indeed of revelation: it makes, for instance, Heinrich Denzinger's Enchiridion of doctrinal definitions and declarations, which first appeared in 1854, into a dogmatic statute-book, beyond discussion, largely dispensing the theologian from critical reflection on the foundations and binding him instead to a sacrifice of intellect.

In practice, then, neo-scholastic Denzinger theology makes Denzinger also the scheme for the structure of systematic theology

as a whole. It provides from these prescribed or condemned propositions a long canon of theses which, from the standpoint of the
Old and New Testament message, represents an utterly arbitrary,
tendentious selection. What fits in is regarded as the Church's
teaching, what does not as not the Church's teaching or simply as
insignificant. No consideration is given either to the perhaps very
different original situation of these documents or to the whole complex history; the effect of the present situation and the attempts to
plan for a better future are also left out of account. The fact that
some of the terms are no longer understood by people of the present time, that the exegetical basis for some propositions is out of
date, that many proofs seem incredible and some answers to questions merely clever humbug—all this is ignored. No one is
bothered about the concrete state of the proclamation. Preacher
and catechist are left in the lurch, given stones instead of bread
and left to find their nourishment just where they can. Thus only
too often the rigid letter rules instead of the spirit and, with a
rapidly changing reality, the mechanical application of the law of
faith finally breaks down and therefore leads to a crisis of faith in
its truth and its truthfulness.

The American Jesuit Father Feeney, with his group, kept faithfully to these principles: he understood the axiom "no salvation
outside" as a law of faith, to be understood literally and therefore
honestly and logically, and—not without an understandable appeal
to the encyclical *Mystici Corporis* of Pius XII—excluded from
salvation all those who do not belong to the organized Catholic
Church. When he would not revoke this, he was excommunicated.
But was he not right? Was he not logical within the scope of a theology that no longer dared to be logical, because this would indeed
be going too far in the world of today? But did this theology, although no longer completely logical, not offer him some comfortable distinctions, with the aid of which he could be traditional and
modern, conservative and progressive in one, which would have
allowed him to assert at the same time both "no salvation outside"
and "salvation outside"? Many theologians asked themselves how a
person could not want to seize on such a comfortable solution. And

in fact any textbook theology which attempts even to a slight degree to come to terms with the difficulties of modern times tends to avoid the difficulties of a purely positivistic interpretation by turning to a "speculative" (it can perhaps be expressed in this way without referring thereby to any particular school of thought). But:

2. A *speculative* interpretation in any sort of form of profession of faith also easily comes into collision with theological truthfulness. The axiom "outside the Church no salvation"—merely a paradigm for many—is then maintained indeed verbally and literally for the sake of a formal orthodoxy, but the whole tenor of the words is reinterpreted. At the same time, the sublime dialectic —on the part of some trained mainly on Aristotle and Thomas Aquinas, of others more on modern philosophy—deserves sincere admiration just as the concern for the unity and continuity of the Church in faith—which frequently finds expression in this interpretation of ecclesiastical creeds, declarations, and definitions—deserves approval.

For a formula is often interpreted dialectically with such brilliant success as to be acceptable to the "orthodox" and "unorthodox." The formula remains (and this is the main thing for the orthodox), but the content is recast (this is what interests the unorthodox). But what does this mean? We cannot but observe that in many cases the text is twisted. At the same time, the formal, conceptual dialectic need not be illogical at all and for the most part it is not. In order to be able to interpret the old formula as if it meant the opposite, it is sufficient if the terms are no longer taken in the same, older sense. To many an unprejudiced observer, who sees through what is not always easy to penetrate, this then certainly seems to contradict historical truth and scientific truthfulness.

In reality, then—to return to the example just mentioned—a theologian like Feeney and other positivistic interpreters are only advised (required, he would say) not to be rigid: the axiom *extra ecclesiam nulla salus* should not be understood primitively, verbally, literally; it must rather be understood intelligently, pneumatically, speculatively, dialectically. And then it means "really" also *extra ecclesiam salus*. It means "really" therefore also its

opposite. In this dialectical operation it is really not at all important which word of the axiom is distinguished, "differentiated":
what is decisive is the result.

We can perhaps make quite clear what sometimes happens in
reality with very much subtle skill and mental expenditure, if we
deliberately caricature the procedure. We can, for example, distinguish *extra* dialectically: *extra* then means really not outside,
but (also) inside (all those who were outside for the early Church,
which coined the axiom, are now inside the Church). Or—and
this is the most frequent starting point of the dialectic—*ecclesia:*
ecclesia then means really not only Church, but (also) the whole
(in good faith) of mankind (the Church is not, as for Origen and
Cyprian—who first used the axiom in its negative form—the organized Church, but all men who live according to their conscience,
honestly convinced atheists too: therefore even those who reject
quite decisively the idea of being members of this Church are
declared against their will, against their explict and implicit *votum,*
"hidden" members of this Church). Or—this distinction too is possible—*salus: salus* really does not mean salvation, but (also)
damnation (even outside, therefore, there is not really damnation,
but only a salvation more difficult to achieve). Or—if we want to
drive the caricature to the limit—*nulla: nulla* really does not
mean "no," but (also) "some" (outside, people are not simply
without salvation, but only without entire salvation; they have only
a part of salvation, since Christian preaching and sacraments are
lacking).

This, however, is enough to show that the speculative interpretation has indeed the right intention in wanting to dissociate itself
from the positivistic understanding of the terms. The formula in
fact no longer suffices in a new speculative situation. And this
kind of speculative dissociation from the original meaning, while
the old formula was still adhered to, was indeed the sole method
that was accepted—or, more accurately, at least tolerated—in the
Catholic theology of the pre-conciliar age. But the fact still cannot
be ignored that the reinterpretation together with the retention of
the same formula is just what renders innocuous the formula itself,

empties it of its original meaning and turns it into its opposite. Thus the procedure leads to an *unwanted* theological untruthfulness, which says "Yes" and "No" simultaneously, frequently leaves the person without theological prejudices perplexed, and in fact leads to ever greater difficulties. In order to present a convincing solution, both the old formulation (in which the positivistic interpretation is interested) and the new intention (to which the speculative interpretation attaches importance), each in its own way, must be taken seriously. And this occurs in the historical interpretation.

3. The *historical* interpretation alone satisfies all the demands of a radical theological truthfulness today. The old formula must not be subtly twisted, distorted in its meaning; the interest of the positivistic interpretation in the old formulation is justified. But at the same time the old formula must not be mechanically repeated, warmed up, for a new situation; the adoption of a new intention by the speculative interpretation is justified. Meanwhile the contrast between the old formulation and the new intention can be resolved only by a new formulation.

Not that the old formulation is to be thrown away on this account: it is a matter of great importance for the Church and theology today to maintain contact with the Church and theology of that time. And therefore to a formula which often throughout very long centuries was the *expression of faith* of our own believing community we shall at all times show respect, attention and reverence. Otherwise, indeed, we could no longer understand our own fathers in the faith. But we can do just that if we understand the old formula as what it really was for its own time. Without speculative re-interpretation or positivistic un-interpretation, it must be soberly understood in the light of the historical situation: of the situation of the theology which shaped it, of the Church in which it lived, of the politics which influenced it, of the civilization which also made its mark upon it; but still more definitely in the light of the situation of the Churches and of the theological parties involved (for example, the Ultramontane party at Vatican I), of the personalities involved (Cyril of Alexandria at Ephesus or Innocent III at the Fourth Lateran Council), nations (the Byzantine Greeks at the earlier councils or the Italians and Spaniards at Trent), schools (Scotism at Trent or Thomism at Vatican I), universities (the Sorbonne at Constance), Orders (the Jesuits at Vatican I), and so on. Thus a formula can really be understood as the result of a quite definite history. Its place in the great and constantly flowing stream of history can be indicated and—finally—it can be questioned critically about its continuity and discontinuity in the light of the binding and authoritative origin of the Church, in the light of the original Christian message itself attested in the Old and New Testament.

Thus it will be possible to do justice even to a formula like "no salvation outside the Church." It had to have another meaning and another function at a time when the *oikumene,* the whole inhabited earth, appeared to include no more than the Mediterranean area with its outskirts and Christendom more or less coincided with mankind. But for an age which, as a result of the discovery of new continents and the study of the long history of mankind, has become conscious of the state of affairs—at first shocking—that Christendom in the light of the past, present and future, in the light of the history of mankind of *all* millennia and *all* continents, is an infinitesimal minority, this axiom has become unintelligible: the expression of a cruel intolerance if it is understood exclusively in the old sense of the world; the expression of a two-faced inconsistency if, according to the formula, no one outside the Catholic Church can be saved and yet, on the other hand, it is not impossible that the greater part of mankind outside the Catholic Church is saved.

Fresh reflection today shows that just this would be in striking contradiction to the gracious saving will of God proclaimed in the gospel of Jesus Christ, for whom there is no *extra,* no outside, but only an *intra,* a within. For this God is not only a God of the Church, but the God of the world "who desires *all* men to be saved and to come to the knowledge of the truth. For there is *one* God, and there is *one* mediator between God and men, the man Christ Jesus, who gave himself as a ransom for *all*" (1 Tim. 2:4–6). The Church, as the community of those who believe in

Christ and acknowledge him, proclaims the salvation of *all* in virtue of Christ's saving deed.

She is the believing, confessing, inviting vanguard of mankind,
knowing by faith what is involved for *all*. But, precisely for the
sake of this faith, she ought no longer to use in her proclamation
the axiom which today has become deceptive and misleading, just
as already—as we know—the Council of Chalcedon (451) no
longer used expressions of the Council of Ephesus (431) which
had become deceptive and misleading. In *theology,* however, for
the sake of continuity with the early Church and of the common
faith, this former expression of faith must be recalled with respect
and reverence, by thinking out on the one hand the positive intention and the true content of the formulation of that time and on the
other its historically conditioned limitation and actual misleading
and unintelligible character. Such a formulation ought to be "com-
memorated" (co-recalled), as in the liturgy a saint is "commemo-
rated" on a day on which a saint of greater importance for the
Church of the present time is to be recalled. Thus the formula
comes into its own, without being able to injure the proclamation
and the pastoral task.[2]

If the Church as a pilgrim Church is constantly on her way, even
in her doctrine; if in the course of history, but also at the same
point of time, many formulations of the one faith are possible in
principle, if the whole truth can never be summed up merely in one
proposition and open-mindedness towards ever greater truth is essential to the Church, then all this still does not mean that the form
of ecclesiastical declarations and definitions is to be constantly
changing. It would be utopian to think that the Church could at any
time begin again at zero with her formulations of faith—still less
carry out a general revision every day. Any kind of business enter-
prise thinks ten times over about the question of whether it should
change the packaging (a little old-fashioned, perhaps) of a well-
established product—alter the legend printed on the wrappings, or
even the name. For it would mean that many would be unable to
recognize the old product in its new form. So much the more will
the Church avoid altering the "packaging, legend or designation" of

her faith without necessity, or still less without reason; but certainly not in order to leave these matters to the whim of the individual.

Ultimately it is a question of what constitutes the basis of existence not only of the individual but of the whole society. And it is not the isolated individual, but the believing community, which is the ultimate authority for the definition of faith in this community. The individual has the right to state his criticism. But he will certainly remain conscious of the danger that his personal formulation may lead him to overstep the Church's frontier—namely, to unbelief. On the other hand, there is nothing to prevent the necessary critical reflection, if its basis is not a fundamental mistrust of ecclesiastical creeds, declarations and definitions, but fundamental trust, allowing for the fact that numerous formulations of the Church's tradition are formulations which have remained faithful to the content of the faith and at the same time intelligible for modern times.

We must also allow for extraordinary situations when the Church and her faith are in dire straits, when it is a question of her very existence and the hour has struck for her to confess her faith (one might recall—for instance—the way in which the so-called "German Christians" compromised with the National Socialist system). Then it may be that a new, binding profession of faith must be defined in a particular form of words, so that the Church with the utmost gravity can bear her witness to the gospel before the world in a final decision. It will then be for the individual and the individual groups not to disturb this common profession, but to give it force. This again does not mean that the Church, particularly in her concern for the common faith, in another situation cannot also renounce a uniform formula and—for the sake of the Church's unity —occasionally even must renounce it (the Council of Florence, for example, refrained from inserting the *Filioque* into the Greek Credo).[3]

Historical interpretation therefore is able to combine reverence for the old with courage for the new, permits us to be critical in virtue of loyalty and loyal in virtue of criticism. But can such historical interpretation overcome all conflicts between the individual's conviction of the faith and the faith of the whole Church? This is the last question that we have to take up here (having often been asked to do so).

Is not a manipulation of the truth inevitable here at least, at any rate if we want to avoid departures from the Church? There is a conflict between faith and faith in which it cannot be decided *a priori* where the superstition, heresy or unbelief lies. Must the Church and her representatives always have been right against the individual? And what of Thomas Aquinas, Savonarola, Galileo and all the theologians condemned in the nineteenth and twentieth centuries? Or is it the other way round? Must the individual always have been right against the Church? And all the real revolutionaries and anarchists—great and small—who, with very dubious motives, attacked the common faith of the Church?

The whole difficulty of the problem complex lies precisely in the fact that in the difficult controversies about faith it cannot be decided *a priori* where the truth lies. As little perhaps as in the case of a physicist who reaches a conclusion, as a result of a series of experiments, that contradicts a generally accepted theory of physics. He may have made a discovery of earth-shaking magnitude, which will force the whole science of physics to change its ideas and which throws a new light on everything: the hitherto unknown man is a second Einstein and a potential Nobel prizewinner. But it may also be otherwise: he may quite simply have made a mistake, and he alone will be the one who has to change his ideas and nothing will come of the Nobel prize. What then will the physicist do in such a case of conflict? He will at least check again and submit all his experiments to renewed, stricter control on all sides. His mistake may indeed be really difficult to discover, but it may also have been in reality an incomprehensible oversight which afterwards makes him tear his hair. In any case, he must be very certain of himself if he wants to go against a "dogma" of physics (the natural sciences, too, have their dogmas, and to call these into question is to court unpopularity). But what does he do if the conflict persists? Will he deny his conclusion solely because it contradicts the general theory? Of course not: that would be a renouncement of truth. Will he put forward his conclusion as absolutely certain and proceed to draw out of it all possible radical consequences? But, after all the testing, his own error is not sufficiently excluded for him to do this; and in science too it is not a good thing to run amok. He will rather consider it as a requirement of his scientific truthfulness—a part of which is also a good dose of modesty—not to be silent, but to present his conclusion for general discussion and wait patiently before he makes his definitive judgment.

It may already have been understood what this example means for the theologian who in his exegetical, historical or systematic investigations reaches a conclusion that does not agree with the faith of the Church as a whole, with some creed, declaration or definition of faith. Such a case of conflict is always possible, not only for the Catholic but also for the non-Catholic theologian, not only in connection with the four Vatican dogmas (papal primacy and infallibility, Mary's immaculate conception and her assumption into heaven) but also in connection with the early councils.

The history of theology shows how there are constantly new questions and how often it is not possible *a priori* to decide where the truth of the gospel lies: some were rightly condemned as heretics, others rehabilitated after their death; some propositions were rightly commended as orthodox, others again after a time rejected in the light of the gospel. Often only the distance of time makes it possible to penetrate a confused situation to a certain extent. The theologian in a case of conflict will therefore test himself above all, his presuppositions, his material, his method, his implications, conclusions and consequences. If he has done this honestly and must abide by his conviction, then he will not be a hypocrite, but hold firmly in truthfulness to the truth he knows and not say— still less write—anything he does not believe. A manipulation of the truth can in no case be considered.

He will not be arrogant on that account, he will not rehearse any revolt, nor direct any ultimatum to the Church or her representative to agree with him on the spot; he will also truthfully continue to allow for a possible mistake or oversight on his part. In complete truthfulness therefore, in this period of unsettled controversy, he will abandon neither his scientific conviction nor the faith of the Church. He will not seek any comfortable solution, as the *terribles simplificateurs* recommend him to do, and he will not in any case sacrifice the one to the other. He knows only too well that for him much more is involved than in a conflict in physical science and that the only thing which will help him and the Church is to venture on the difficult walk along the ridge between two precipices and to endure the conflict. He will therefore be neither silent nor mutinous. He will be neither intimidated nor be goaded on. He will neither permit his "obedience" to be exploited nor ever forget his place in the community of faith. He will neither retract what he knows to be true nor revolt against the Church. He will rather express his view in the right way and before the right public—both are important—and he will enter into the discussion fearlessly and with a detached serenity, waiting patiently before making his definitive judgment—it could be a long time. And in the course of time it will become clear where the truth lies: with him, with the Church, or—there are so many half-truths—with both.

So the truth of this theologian will prevail perhaps at a very late stage. But because of this it will prevail without a new schism, it will prevail in the *whole* Church. And this ought to be important for any theologian as a member of the community of faith. This ought to make his patient waiting bearable. Or is there anyone still today who thinks it would be worth while—instead of this—to found a new Church for a newly discovered truth?

Luther is to be excused because this is not what he wanted to do. He was already excluded at the beginning of the discussion, excommunicated by those who lived in another world (Renaissance) and understood notoriously little of his theological concerns, and thus the disaster of schism took its course. Today, in view of the depressing progress of the divisions of Protestantism, it ought to be clear to any theologian that it has no meaning for him and is no solution for the Church to take the risk again of a new schism for the sake of a newly discovered truth or to set himself apart as an individual. Neither excommunication by the Church nor withdrawal from the Church is the right solution of the conflict here. The right solution is rather patient and courageous wrestling with the difficulties, mutual tolerance and a common quest for the whole truth in radical truthfulness within the Church. No manipulation of truth, but "speaking the truth in love" (Eph. 4:15).

NOTES

1. Cf. DS 76, 468-9, 792, 802, 870-875, 1051, 1351, 1868-1870, 2540, 2730-2732, 2865, 2916-2918, 3302-4. Not in Denzinger-Schönmetzer, but in earlier editions of Denzinger (brought up to date by Karl Rahner) cf. 1646f., 2199, 2319. (It is interesting to note that this last reference—omitted by Schönmetzer—is to *Humani Generis,* where Pius XII identifies the mystical body with the Roman Catholic Church [Trans].)

2. Cf., with reference to the further consequences in the relationship between the Church and world-religions: "Christenheit als Minderheit" (*Theol. Med.* 12, Einsiedeln, 1965).

3. For the dogma, cf. W. Kasper, *Dogma unter dem Wort Gottes* (Mainz, 1965).

IX/Outlook

THE FUTURE of truthfulness has already begun in the Church. The numerous *demands* of this book would be misunderstood if they were taken *merely* as demands and not at the same time also to a gratifying extent as *realizations,* which call for further realization. The truthful Church is not pure music of the future.

How would it have been possible in connection with Vatican II to bring about this radical change, this amazing new sense for truthfulness in the Church, if so much had not already been prepared before the Council? John XXIII, a charismatic in the Petrine office, struck the spark of a new truthfulness in the Church. But how could it have been ignited unless already, long before the Council, people known and unknown had been working up the material that turned the spark into a fire?

Already, long before the conciliar breakthrough, there were in fact numerous witnesses of a new truthfulness. The sufferings of these pioneers of a new truthfulness were not slight. And we younger ones, standing on their shoulders and having it so much easier in many respects, we must not forget this. We have every reason to respect the Christian commitment of those lonely heroes in a struggle for a new truthfulness, a future of the Church which seemed then to have very little prospect. They groaned under the untruthfulness, weakness, obscurity and unholiness of the holy Church of God for which all their work was done—but they did not leave her. They suffered under faulty developments and faulty attitudes which had slipped into proclamation and teaching, worship and pastoral care, church order and piety, into relations with other Christians and with the world—but they did not give up. They were suspected, hindered, disavowed, calumniated, persecuted and exiled, by fellow-Christians, by bishops and theologians in the Church—but they continued to work as best they could. They were considered dangerous, extremist, too radical, heretical-revolutionary; but they went on, as far as they were allowed to go and sometimes beyond this: doggedly patient, fearless and bold against all fear, often in an obedience that seemed like disobedience to superiors, since they obeyed God rather than men.

As theologians or worker-priests, as priests in the parish or committed lay people, they stood in the front line of fire, mostly without human protection, backed only by the gospel of Jesus Christ. Often only after decades, sometimes too only after their death, were they publicly thanked for it; some of them were rehabilitated only by the Second Vatican Council. And thus their suffering—without excusing those who created it—became grace. The Lord, who remains faithful to his Church, did not permit the ruin of the hope to which they held against all hope. What was begun modestly and unobtrusively by individuals, what came to prevail slowly and painfully, has now in many respects been realized: in the renewal of theology, of liturgy, of Church-life altogether, in encounter with the other Christian Churches, with world-religions, with the modern secular world. And it became clear that those pioneers of a new truthfulness were not outsiders, but the vanguard of a main force, following indeed slowly but at heart willingly, compared to which some official representatives in theology and church government proved more and more to be a rearguard.

This became clear anyway only through the Council. Here the hour of truthfulness struck, not only for those solitary and unappreciated individuals but for the whole Catholic Church, and indirectly also for all Christendom. Of course, not everything can be attained at one stroke. And, even where something might have been achieved at once (for example, the introduction of the vernacular in the whole liturgy and so on), bishops largely preferred to go "step by step" across a brook that might have been crossed in a bold leap without getting wet feet. And, as a result of such a little-planned gradual approach, there was no little disorder and loss of authority, and at the same time frequently it was possible neither to convince those who held back nor to curb those thrusting forward.

Nevertheless, in spite of all hesitation, hindrance, resistance, a new truthfulness has already become established to an amazing extent in the Catholic Church: particularly at the parish level with some priests and lay people, but more and more among theologians and bishops in the greater church organizations, and not only at the outposts of the Church but also in some Roman offices. There is now so much gratifying progress in the Church. And so many a point expressed in this book in the form of a challenging imperative, in regard to many an individual, many a parish and many a group, in spite of persistent human weaknesses, may be formulated gratefully in the indicative. Here there not only ought to be, there *is* already a Church which in truthfulness knows what she does not know; here *is* already a Church which—particularly in her weakness, ignorance and fallibility—trusts imperturbably in God's grace, fidelity and truth, and which just so is certain of her faith, happy, strong and critically self-critical; here *is* already a Church full of mental spontaneity, vitality, fruitfulness, capacity for love, a Church which gladly listens to new questions, which is able to appreciate relevant and specialist knowledge, modern methods, observations and results; a Church which has courage for initiative and risk, which is wholly and entirely open to reality. In a word: here, in these individuals, in these parishes and groupings, there *is* already in a new fashion a truthful Church.

And where there is now already a truthful Church, on a small scale and occasionally too on a large scale, then this Church can also proclaim truth in a new way for the men of this age, truth which can give a meaning to human life. And this we need today.

For a time in our highly civilized states it seemed that man could be helped by the realization of his social and cultural demands, cherished for decades and centuries. But in America and Europe now, what is the basic attitude of so many sons and daughters of those fathers who had to struggle doggedly and ambitiously in order to have enough money, a house of their own, a car, every luxury? They accept more or less gratefully and naturally the precious results of their elders' untiring struggle. But just because they no longer have this before them as the goal of a struggle, as their fathers did, but possess it without having had to fight for it, they are asking about the meaning of the whole, which has fallen to their lot and cannot be a goal any longer. And particularly the most truthful among them frequently question the values, the meaning of things. And the end—at least provisional—of this quest is in not all-too-rare cases complete futility.

Is this surprising? The reality of the "secular city," as it is experienced, is all too contradictory. Its anonymity, its mobility, its bureaucratic organization, but also the new secularized theories of work, of sexuality, of education, are liberating, humanizing to a high degree; man has become articulate, responsible, to an astonishing extent. After Bonhoeffer and Gogarten, Harvey Cox has made a considerable impression on theologians too, so that they see this in a new light.

Theology, for its higher ends, does not need to depreciate anything that is good in itself. But the same anonymity, mobility and bureaucratic organization of the "secular city" allows innumerable human beings to perish inwardly—and often also outwardly. It is precisely the scientists who claim that the character of chance clings to the fantastic progress of technical civilization; we have been hearing, of late, about the irrationality of the dynamism of civilization and the uncontrolled second technological revolution. The contradictions of the "experiment man" are becoming still more evident and frequent in the technopolis. The contradictions of a society which, in an unparalleled triumph of technology, reaches for the stars and yet is still not capable of solving the most primitive problems of the earth: peace, hunger, slums, the abysmally deep contrast between the haves and have nots, white and colored, north and south, and all the diverse forms of man's inhumanity to man.

The theologian in particular must not permit his rationalistic optimism to blind him to the results of sociological criticism since Marx. But the contradictions too of human existence, of a human being who is able to control everything except himself, whose power again and again is turned into arbitrariness, knowledge into stupidity, goodness into appalling egoism; whose physical capacity and moral responsibility present such a striking contrast; whose civilized perfectionism is constantly faced by new sufferings and finally by invincible death: death which, for every human life, renders all attainment dubious from the very beginning. Nor is it possible particularly for the theologian to overlook the findings of psychological criticism since Freud.

Is there really any meaning to the whole thing? As early as the time of the First World War the Jew Franz Kafka was writing in lonely isolation with a vision beyond that of his contemporaries. In his stories and novels, part of which were published after his death and contrary to his expressed will, he described in painfully vivid, realist-symbolist truthfulness what were to prove the most profound anxieties and fears of man in the welfare society of the second half of the twentieth century: the man who in the mechanization, the routine and the complexity of modern life no longer knows where he belongs; who feels that he is at the mercy of authorities, anonymous powers ruling the world in a hidden way yet everywhere present; who suffers from uprootedness and estrangement in which even love between fellow human beings no longer offers any real alleviation; one who can no longer discover any meaning in the paradox of human life.

Is it not this situation which finds expression in the mental irritability of so many intellectuals, in unrest in the universities, in the resignation or rebellion of so many advanced students? Fear, despair, hopelessness in a completely organized world, apparently well equipped with everything, but in which man seeks in vain for genuine dignity, love, forgiveness, fulfilment; in which there is only the logic of the absurd, in which the only thing that is not in doubt is the dubiousness of human existence, the perception of nothingness as the ultimate reality: Is this not the basic mood in the light of which philosophers like Sartre or writers like Camus, Beckett,

Ionesco and other representatives of the theater of the absurd analyze our time and grasp it perhaps more intuitively than so many optimistic politicians and wielders of power?

In spite of all the bustle and talking, a waiting that goes round in circles, without content, without direction, without aim, without meaning: How many human beings are "waiting for Godot," just as in Samuel Beckett's play, in spite of all outward movement, in an inward stagnation full of boredom, of weariness of life and of futility, waiting for something, someone who is always going to come and yet does not come? Where is there an answer? An answer to the unsolved problem of guilt, to man's "original sin" of being born, to the question—never finally to be silenced, forgotten, suppressed—of the great whence and whither, why and to what purpose? What is truth?

Behind all these questions is there, in the background, only chance or the necessity of nothingness? No matter how much they appear, and are intended to appear in detail, as one-sided caricatures—as bizarre, grotesque, absurd—the analyses of thinkers and poets nevertheless reveal to man his really ominous situation, seek to dislodge him from his conformist self-satisfaction and boredom, and unmask as untruth what is not truth in modern life.

And however much the disturbances and revolts of students and scholars may exhibit in detail terrorist and fascist or even merely irritating and infantile features, they are the clinical thermometer of society and expose the untruthfulness of modern society and its frequently hypocritical morality and politics. These young people are not willing to be alienated, dehumanized, delivered up to anonymous bureaucracies, mechanisms and social forces, to the agencies of the Establishment. "There comes a moment when the working of the machine becomes so cruel, when one becomes so sick, so disheartened, that it is simply impossible to co-operate any longer—not even to take part in silence. Then you have to throw yourselves on the gears and wheels, on the levers and all this equipment and bring it to a halt. And you must make clear to the people responsible for the machine and the people to whom it belongs that it will never again work at all, unless you become free."

The rebellion of the American students of Berkeley began with these words of Mario Savio on the campus of the University of California in 1964. Is this not the breakthrough of an elemental protest against a hopelessly technicized, bureaucratized world, robbed of its ultimate meaning: an elemental quest in radical truthfulness for truth, for meaning?

And who could help here? The Yogi, who turns away from all activity and takes refuge in contemplation, or LSD? The realities of modern life are too harsh and too solid to be resolved in either way. Or, as the other extreme, the political agitator who is not afraid of using any kind of force to establish his better order? Everywhere, according to the analysis of Camus, or of Peter Weiss as described in the total hopelessness of his *Marat,* terrorism is impending. Everywhere there is the menace of terrorism, either of the individual or the state—the irrational terrorism of fascism or the rational terrorism of Marxism, dictatorship or anarchy. And have not the quasi-religions of nationalism and communism conclusively shown what the results are if the national or the social factor is made into an ultimate claim, to which everything else must be subordinated?

Neither the values of the nation, the Fatherland, the people or the race, nor those of the class, the proletariat, the international, are rated so highly today as to constitute an ultimate meaning of life for men in the leading states of East and West. And in this sense it is not necessarily a sign of retrogression if youth no longer have "ideals" of this kind: that is perhaps why they no longer so readily permit themselves to be misused. Yet it cannot be overlooked that even the *ratio* of the Enlightenment, even modern science and technology, psychology and sociology, even politics cannot answer the ultimate questions about the meaning of the whole, about the whence and whither, the why and the wherefore of it all. And any form of a humanistic (or political) faith in science leads only to new (and often amazingly romantic) utopias, ideologies and terminologies, without being able to put a stop to alienation and bureaucratization, to the anonymous forces, the conformism and untruthfulness of the world.

Naturally, it would likewise be illusory utopian thinking to suppose that the Church can solve all these problems. Problems of humanity, like those of master and servant, right and power, individual and institution, freedom and order, simply cannot be solved "once and for all." Untruthfulness, mendacity, lying and fraud will remain in the world. Naturally, distorted reality must be altered wherever it is found, the world must be made human by every means: in particular, aid must constantly be given to the ruled against the ruler, to right against all might and power, to the individual against the over-powerful institution, to the dignity and freedom of man against the anonymous bureaucracy, organization and manipulation of the Establishment. But questions already solved are succeeded by new ones (often only the old in a new form), and only a romantic believer in progress or a totally utopian Marxist can hope for a perfect human society in this world, in which the principle "to each according to his needs, from each according to his abilities" would be the rule.

Wherever on a great or small scale—with individuals or groups —there is a truthful Church, such a Church is able to proclaim truth, present truth to man, which can give his life a direction, a content, a goal, a meaning. This Church does not put man off with a "hereafter," but directs him to the present: to take up actively his responsibility here and now in the world. But she shows him at the same time the reason for his responsibility: her message puts bounds to his fear, repels his despair, conquers his hopelessness.

A truthful Church does not give man any cheap recipes for his private life, and still less for world politics in its different forms. But it gives man ground under his feet, letting him know about his whence and whither, his why and to what purpose. This knowledge is not the knowledge of the ascertaining, arguing reason, which plainly reaches its limits in these questions and—if overstrained —leads to total scepticism. This knowledge is the knowledge of trusting and understanding faith, which is a venture, a risk, an experiment, as indeed love and hope too are always a venture, experiment and risk, which cannot be demonstrated by reason. But this trusting and understanding faith can give to the person who ventures on it deeper certainty, greater power, more far-reaching hope and mightier love than all arguments of pure reason.

Wherever with individuals or groups there is a truthful Church, there occurs in the midst of the world remote from God the miracle of experiencing God's presence: man knows with absolute certainty that he is not thrown from nothingness into nothingness, that in all the uncertain wavering, in all almost blind groping and all desperate seeking, he has a support on which he can rely—in every affliction, in every error and every lapse. He knows then—even in all his detours, digressions and false trails—whence he really comes, where in principle he stands, whither he is finally going: that God in fact is his source, his way and his goal, and that responsibility before God makes him also take with full seriousness his responsibility in the world for men.

Wherever a parish priest preaches well, straightforwardly and genuinely; wherever an individual, a family or a parish sincerely and seriously prays, without set phrases; wherever baptism is carried out in the right Spirit, in the name of Christ; wherever the Eucharist of a committed community is celebrated in a way that is effective in ordinary life: wherever forgiveness of sin is granted, incomprehensibly, by God's power; wherever in the service of God and the service of men, in instruction and pastoral care, in discussion and works of charity, the gospel is preached, exemplified and followed in a truthful way: all this constitutes the imitation of Christ. Man learns something of the real reason for his loneliness, abandonment and decay in this world, for his uncanny fear, anxiety and despair; but he learns also of the real reason for the possibility of a radical change, redemption, renewal and fulfilment; he perceives the fatality and promise of sin that finds forgiveness, the nonsense and sense of suffering which can be overcome, the darkness and radiance of death that means fulfilment; a way is constantly opened afresh to man, so that he has light at least sufficient for the next step, so that today he will at least do somewhat better than yesterday, so that his love is ever greater than his scepticism;

he develops a new freedom for the tasks which face him, the human beings who live with him, for the joy that surprises him, the bitter sufferings that come upon him.

Wherever there is a truthful Church, there is discussion, comprehension, communication and mental expansion; by God's Spirit and power, timidity and insecurity, constriction and calcification, fanaticism and resentment, hypocrisy and inactivity, fade out; freedom and joy begin to prevail, magnanimity and generosity, broad-mindedness and tolerance, lovableness and brotherliness, courage, self-confidence, commitment, humor, hope and trust in truth: all this as a testimony before God who so plainly is present and operative where he seems to be absent, who is sustaining the life of the world while the world is proclaiming his death.

Wherever with individuals or groups there is a truthful Church, a necessary demythologizing and de-demonizing occurs, a deepening and humanizing of the world and man; there is something like a dawning of that complete justice, that eternal life, that cosmic peace, that true freedom and that final reconciliation of mankind with God which one day God's consummated kingdom will bring. And must all this be without significance for the world's structures, leaving them undisturbed in their autonomy? must it be without importance for science, economy, politics, state, society, law and culture? Even though—precisely for the sake of truthfulness—this Church, as Church, avoids an intervention for which she is not competent in the great and small daily questions of the world, in which the gospel of Jesus Christ is not unambiguously and clearly involved, this truthful Church is still able to produce people who can undertake responsibility in all these great and small, daily questions of the world, in a new maturity, autonomy, superiority and freedom, so that in his dominion over the world man remains human in the truth, subject to the dominion of God. And must it not be possible for the hope of such men, for such an open, mobile, hospitable community, to have a contagious influence? Must it not be able to change the status quo and to share in leading to a better future of the world?

This truthful Church is not merely a project. She is a reality which innumerable people live. From outside, she can be perceived only to a limited extent. The fact that she exists we must believe from what we are told by those who have known her. And a person who himself wants to know her cannot escape the venture of a commitment.

The truthfulness which exists in the Church calls for that which could exist. The truthful Church calls for the conversion of the untruthful. This is something that we must not imagine in an oversimple way: for we ourselves, I myself, constantly belong to the truthful *and* untruthful Church; and this conversion is constantly required from ourselves, from myself. In the Church nothing is done without the individual, without the truthfulness of the heart. But the individual must be helped. And therefore—precisely in view of the heart of the individual—the renewal is needed of ecclesiastical institutions and constitutions, of structures and contours. And so that we shall not be remaining on a high academic plane, without commitment in the distress of the time, with regard to the demands made in our first section in line with the trend of the Second Vatican Council, we shall indicate here some possibilities and necessities in reforming the institutional Church, which alone can lead to the truthful Church of the future.

The theological foundations for the reforms, some of them farreaching, have been set forth in my book *The Church* and must be presupposed here. There is no need to insist on the fact that it is a question merely of suggestions, any more than on the fact that this is nothing other than a summary of what has been discussed and desired by many and makes no claim to originality. The proposals must be understood rather as the suggestions made in *The Council, Reform and Reunion* (1960–61), when the Council was in prospect, were understood; in a gratifying way, many were allowed to be fulfilled by the Council.

These suggestions for the further structural reform of the postconciliar Church will not win universal agreement at once. They should be objectively *discussed*. They are not intended to form a balanced whole, but to establish the main points. They are not meant to be complete, but to set out what is of immediate importance. They are not intended to deal with what is theoretically possible, but to suggest a concrete plan of action. The discussion will bring to light further suggestions and new shifts of emphasis: certain complex questions need deeper and more comprehensive elaboration. Yet all this should not keep us from the immediate *action* for which so many are waiting with the utmost impatience. Here a deliberate choice has been made mainly of those suggestions which it is possible to begin at once to realize.

A. GENERAL TASKS RESULTING FROM THE COUNCIL

1. Execution of the Council decrees in the individual countries:

A realization, not according to the letter which kills, but according to the spirit which gives life. For this a broad, systematic consultation and clear, considered, courageous planning are indispensable, and to this in turn there is presupposed a free discussion of the different questions among the competent representatives of the different groups.

Episcopal commissions whose membership is not published and which meet away from the light of publicity in the Church can hardly be regarded as the right means: in many cases they are too esoteric-hierarchical, too lacking in competence and only too often insufficiently representative of the whole people of God, among whom (as, for instance, on questions of the Catholic schools or celibacy) other views prevail than those of the bishops and the people they prefer as advisers. *Quod omnes tangit, ab omnibus tractari debet,* "what touches all must be agreed by all," so runs an ancient principle of the Church's law. Collegiality must not remain merely a claim on the Roman central office, but must be realized at all levels. It will not work without the co-operation of bishops, parish priests, curates, theologians and lay people in all spheres of the Church's life.

A good model for the planning and execution of the Church's renewal in the different countries is provided by the Dutch pastoral council (national synod). Here, with a lay chairman, bishops, theologians and lay people from the most diverse classes and callings (70 of the 107 voting members of the pastoral council are from the laity), along with representatives of the other Christian Churches and of non-Christians, deliberate and make decisions freely and openly about the realization of reform in that country (the question of authority and of office in the Church occupied the first place in the discussions). The Dutch pastoral council in its thematic, personal and organizational preparation is distinguished in a very pleasing way from the first Roman synod of bishops (1967), which is scarcely to be counted as a great success. Here— as in some post-conciliar episcopal conferences also—through an intention that was quite transparent, both in the preparation and in the execution, theological experts and certain burning issues (celibacy, birth-regulation) were excluded.

2. General renewal of theology:

An urgent need has developed today for a total renewal of theology on a solid exegetical, historical, systematic and ecumenical basis in the light of the conditions which face the Church in the world at the present time: the matter cannot be dealt with here. A renewal of theology cannot simply be "decreed." Theology in the strict sense cannot be produced by a "magisterium," but only by theologians. Theology is a science, differentiated into many special fields, which must make use of quite definite and delicate methods of research. The Council particularly requires Catholic theology to make a fresh effort to start out again from the original Christian message; but much time will be needed before Scripture is again the "soul of theology" in a form appropriate to the age. Meanwhile, in regard to structural reform, two urgent desiderata must be stated:

a. Theology must be given complete freedom, in order to fulfil its task with both critical discernment and ecclesial commitment. For this reason the last of the censorship measures left over from an absolutist age must be promptly abolished, particularly the precensoring of theological books (*imprimatur*), which has indirectly done great damage to the Church.

b. Between bishops and teachers, *pastores et doctores,* in the

Church, each of whom have their specific function, there must be a trustful *co-operation*. Hence, in the spirit of Cardinal Döpfner's suggestions at the synod of bishops: the convocation in Rome of a commission of theologians from all countries to advise the pope and the Congregation for the Doctrine of the Faith (agreed on by the synod of bishops); the setting up of a committee of theologians at every bishops' conference; consultation between the pope and the bishops' conferences before the publication of important documents. The composition of a catalogue of errors, of a "rule of faith" or of a universal "catechism," demanded by curial circles, is absolutely useless for the present situation.

3. Consistent carrying out of liturgical reform:

In principle liturgical reform is on the right track and already most satisfactorily advanced. With the consent of Rome the vernacular has come to prevail throughout the liturgy within a very short time—far beyond what the Council envisaged. The great danger, however, is not so much the possibility of a wild growth (which scarcely weighs in the balance against the still widespread traditional stagnation) as that of a renewed ritualization, fixation and rubricizing of the Mass. In order to secure in the liturgy the vitality, mobility, variety that it still lacks in spite of the use of the vernacular and many simplifications, to secure the necessary adaptation to the time and concentration on essentials, it will be necessary to go beyond what has been decided in a number of ways:

a. Instead of translated Latin prayers, there must be prayers shaped in content and language by the present time, prayers which may also be partly formulated spontaneously; as many modern canons of the Mass as possible, theologically sound and linguistically well shaped, with the New Testament account of the institution of the Eucharist.

b. Instead of two or even three ritualized readings, there should be possible merely one—occasionally somewhat lengthier—reading from Scripture, which in any case is to be briefly and attractively interpreted. In weekday Masses the continuous reading of a freely chosen book of the Bible (*lectio continuata*) should be permitted, always with a brief, concentrated interpretation in the light of a modern commentary.

c. Communion under both kinds should be made possible, even in the ordinary parish Mass (in a simple and hygienic form, with each communicant taking for himself the bread presented on the paten and dipping it into the chalice).

d. There should be hymns which textually and vocally are—in the best sense of the words—modern and popular.

e. There should be the possibility of absolution even apart from private confession, in the celebration of the Eucharist or in special services of penance.

f. Anachronistic devotions should be abolished and appropriate forms of prayer should replace those which are obsolete, even for priests.

4. Basic reform of Canon Law:

A good reform particularly of Canon Law, for which a Roman commission was created, is inconceivable without the widest possible discussion and consultation: in the decisive commission, in addition to the canonists, there are needed not only theological and sociological experts, but also priests engaged in practical, pastoral work and a strong international contingent of laymen and lay women, and—finally (as also in the liturgical commission)—observers from the other Christian Churches. The work of reform must not be dominated—as hitherto—largely by the machinery and mentality of the Roman Curia—which is essentially not a legislative but an administrative body—nor may it take place in secret; it must be accounted for publicly in the Church. Canon law urgently needs to be stripped of its mystification and ideology. The norm in every case must be the gospel of Jesus Christ itself, the foundation a biblical ecclesiology.

Hence a *total* revision of the code is necessary, in structure, form, content and orientation; at the same time what should be sought is not at all a closed, unchangeable, systematic code, but an open, constantly adaptable canon law (before 1918 there was no such code). Canon Law must never be a sum of sovereign rights but always a law of service and, as such, fundamentally a living law, constantly open to revision, so that human beings are not caught in the law, but are helped by the law: a law of grace, expressive therefore of brotherliness and of the fundamental equality of all Christians.

By resistance to all juridicizing, bureaucratizing and clericalizing of the Church, the freedom of the sons and daughters of God must be not only preserved but promoted by the law through a minimum of legal regulation: as much freedom as possible, as much obligation as necessary, and not the opposite. In the light of this formulation of the principle of subsidiarity, it would be appropriate today to strike out the greater part of the existing canons.

The "guide lines" of the commission on the Code do in fact express what is basic to the reform of Canon Law, but this is scarcely taken with sufficient and consistent seriousness:

a. The juridical character of the Code, which requires only legal norms, regulating the common life of the community, to be adopted and not dogmatic and moral provisions.

b. The distinction of a universal "basic order" destined for the whole Church, limited to essentials and ecumenically oriented; then of "regional orders," ordinances of more limited scope, holding for the larger spheres of the Church (continents, different cultural spheres, the Eastern Church); finally of "national or diocesan orders," detailed ordinances, holding for particular nations or dioceses (administrative regulations).

c. Emphasis and protection of personal basic rights (human rights, legal protection against the arbitrariness of ecclesiastical administration, rights of the laity, guarantee also of the right to information in the Church, and so on).

d. Clear separation of legislative, administrative and judicial powers.

e. Comprehensive decentralization in the spirit of the principle of subsidiarity (especially positive restriction of papal and episcopal reservations to what is absolutely necessary; general dismantling of the system of dispensations).

f. Radical reduction of penal law (excommunication, etc.) and revision of legal procedure (publicity, speeding up particularly of marriage processes, administrative jurisdiction).

A consultation of the other Christian Churches before promulgating a new basic order ought today to be self-evident from the ecumenical standpoint. For the rest, in this transitional situation, haste is required: certainly in regard to work on the basic questions, but not in regard to the formulation of new canons (amazingly enough, the commission has already again prepared in rough outline about 383 canons, although the basic questions can by no means be regarded as clarified).

B. SPECIAL TASKS OF REFORM IN REGARD TO THE CHURCH'S CONSTITUTION:

1. Members of the Church or their representatives must have a voice in the affairs of the local, diocesan, national and universal Church (but also in religious orders). Authoritarian one-man government, supported neither by the original New Testament constitution of the Church nor by present-day democratic thinking, must be replaced by a collegial government of the Church at all levels: parish, diocese, nation, whole Church. There should be a good system of checks and balances. The final authority of the parish priest, bishop, pope, should be expressly maintained in order to avoid a general paralysis of the different forces. But at the same time the representative bodies should be assured not only of a part in debates but also of a share in decisions. It is decisive for the representative character of these bodies that the majority of the members (men and women) should be chosen by free and secret voting: a minority can become a member *ex officio* or through the appointment of the responsible ministry (parish priest, bishop, bishops' conference, pope), especially if someone performs certain important functions in the community. The constitutional foundations for these reforms have been laid to a considerable extent by the Council itself.

a. For every *diocese* a senate of priests was prescribed, and in many places one has already been formed. The freely elected

senate of priests represents the presbyterium of the diocese, in order to give effective support to the bishop in the administration of
the diocese. Likewise a diocesan pastoral council, consisting of
priests, religious and laity, was prescribed by Vatican II, and this
too has been already realized in part (the senate of priests being
for the most part integrated into the pastoral council, in which the
laity might sometimes have a two-thirds majority).

b. For every *parish,* where it has not yet been set up, there
should be an elected parish council, corresponding to the diocesan
pastoral council, to share in debates and decisions on all important parochial affairs.

c. For every *nation,* again corresponding to the above-men-
tioned diocesan pastoral council and as a result of a national
pastoral assembly, there should be established a permanent national pastoral council, consisting of bishops, priests and lay people, to share in debates and decisions on all important national
ecclesiastical affairs.

d. For the *whole Church,* parallel to the council of bishops already constituted (but not yet permanent and assembling periodically) and as a result of the international congress of laity, there
should be established a lay council which—together with the council of bishops, under the final direction of the pope—debates and
decides about important matters affecting the whole Church. At all
levels theological and other experts must be brought in.

2. There should be free election of the appropriate superiors
(parish priests, bishop, pope) by representatives of the Churches
concerned. This both with the co-operation of the representative
bodies mentioned in the last point, in the whole Church (council
of bishops and lay council), in the diocese (pastoral council) and in
the local Church (parish council), and also with the superordinate
pastoral ministry exercising a controlling and approving function:
the bishop for the election of a parish priest, the conference of
bishops or the pope for the election of a bishop. As far as the election of the pope is concerned, it is a matter of special urgency that
this should be handed over by the college of cardinals—which is
in no way representative and is in any case an anachronism—to

the council of bishops and the lay council. All appointments to ecclesiastical positions should be governed analogously by the principles: "No bishop shall be appointed against the will of the people" (Pope Celestine I) and "The one who will be at the head of all must be chosen by all" (Pope Leo the Great). Election for a long but limited time (for example, six or eight years with a possibility of re-election) should be seriously considered in the present situation, not only for superiors or superioresses of religious orders, or—as in certain parts of the Church—for the parish priest, but for all office-holders.

Directives for obligatory (e.g., at seventy) or facultative (e.g., at sixty-five) retirement from ecclesiastical office are necessary. On the other hand, no demand of a parish for the retirement of the holder of a ministry should have the force of law without the consent of the ministry set above this (bishop for parish priest, pope for bishop): thus illegitimate attempts to exercise pressure on an incumbent can be repelled. A special committee should advise the bishop in all personnel matters: this committee in all cases should weigh very precisely the special peculiarities and requirements of the post in question and also the wishes of the person involved. At the same time, particular attention must be given to the relationships between parish priest and curates—where so much is wrong.

3. Theological, legal, sociological and psychological overhauling of the traditional "priest"-image: celibacy in the Church's ministry —as it has always been in the Eastern Churches united with Rome, so too again in the Latin Church—should be left to the free decision of the individual in the light of his personal vocation. There should be definite regulations about clerical dress only in relation to religious services. There should be general reform of prelates' dress and titles and also of the religious habit; replacement of the Tridentine seminary training by a spiritual formation appropriate to the time in the college style.

4. Open budgeting and presentation of accounts of the use of church monies in parish, the nation, and the Church as a whole is essential. Policy-making and budgetary decisions are inevitably linked.

5. There should be consistent execution of the reforms undertaken in the structure and personnel of the Roman Curia: internationalizing, decentralizing, dismantling of the inflated bureaucratic machinery; abandonment of the absolutist style in government and speech; re-examination of the necessity of secular diplomacy (nuncios, etc.), together with the abolishing of anachronistic Vatican court titles and awards of orders which have nothing to do with the Church of Christ (and which were not abolished even by most recent laudable reforms).

6. A more rational division of dioceses (as required by the Council) is necessary, but also a (preliminary or subsequent) fundamental decentralization and reorganization of dioceses: instead of auxiliary bishops without special responsibility in the episcopal city, ordained local bishops (without pontifical titles and ornate dress) in the important centers, to relieve the diocesan bishop for Confirmation, co-ordinating functions, etc., so that the diocesan bishop as the real metropolitan may devote himself to his proper tasks (pastoral care for the priests in the parishes, care of the formation, distribution and rational use of priests, thorough visitation of parishes, co-ordination of pastoral work at the regional and national levels, taking part in the governing of the Church as a whole). At the same time, the diocesan bishop—with the reduction in diocesan responsibility—will need above all a "brains trust" of experts, varying with the diverse problems, not necessarily domiciled in the episcopal city.

7. New determination of the structure and functions of the *parish* is essential: activation of the whole congregation; adaptation to the specific needs and requirements of the area covered by the parish; concentration on essential pastoral tasks, and thence too appropriate assistance in mastering decisive problems of the village or town parish concerned; encouragement of smaller, free groupings—not necessarily limited to parochial boundaries—with a diversity of objectives; Mass, not only in the parish church, but—especially on weekdays—also in private houses for groups from the neighborhood.

8. There should be an upgrading of woman's position in the

Church: full participation of women in the life of the Church, on the basis of equal rights; qualified women in all the deciding bodies described above, from the parish council to the lay senate of the whole Church; training and enlistment of women for an active share in responsibility at the different levels; promotion of theological studies for women and also of a corresponding theological teaching activity; revision of the numerous liturgical texts and canons of ecclesiastical law which discriminate against women; admission of deaconesses and serious examination of the concrete conditions for ordaining women, against which no biblical or dogmatic arguments can be raised.

9. There should be reform of religious communities in the Church for the requirements of the present time, in accordance with the message of Christ (and not with the ascetic standards of the Qumran community of the Dead Sea). New interpretation is necessary of the "evangelical counsels": "celibacy" (what cannot be a universal law for the Church's ministry makes sense particularly for a religious community at the service of their fellow-men); "poverty" (community administration of the incomes of the members does not exclude a personal budget for personal expenses); "obedience" (not blind obedience; respect for personal dignity and the freedom of all members; in small communities, instead of "superiors," more teamwork with a *primus inter pares*). There should be theological investigation as to whether religious vows are necessary at all, or to what extent: the same religious commitment might in any case be realized in different ways in the same community (members with diverse obligations: no vows at all, voluntary temporary vows, voluntary vows for an indeterminate period, maintenance of the connection of former members with the community). There should be the greatest possible freedom for each community to shape its own life (life of prayer, work, recreation, administration, clothing).

C. SPECIAL TASKS CONTRIBUTING TO ECUMENICAL UNDERSTANDING BETWEEN THE DIFFERENT CHRISTIAN CHURCHES

1. Unreserved mutual recognition of baptisms.

2. Regular exchange of preachers, catechists and professors of theology for mutual appreciation of common interests and tasks to be carried out together.

3. More frequent, and not merely exceptional, common ecumenical services of the word, as already permitted, and examination of the conditions for common eucharistic services.

4. Greater freedom to take part in services in other Christian Churches (especially for mixed marriages).

5. Greatest possible common use of churches and common reconstruction of churches and presbyteries.

6. Settlement of the mixed marriage problem by recognizing the validity of all mixed marriages and leaving the decision on baptism and education of the children to the conscience of the marital partners. (Ecumenical marriage ceremony.)

7. Promotion of common biblical study in the parishes (common translations and commentaries).

8. A strengthening of co-operation and integration between confessional theological faculties (merger of seminary libraries, common teaching arrangements).

9. Examination of the possibilities of a common theological-ecumenical basic course of study.

10. Ecumenical co-operation in public life (adoption of an agreed position, common initiatives and campaigns).

D. SPECIAL TASKS IN THE SERVICE OF THE MODERN WORLD

1. A general reconsideration of the Church's commitment in the world, best carried out at the national or regional level: overcommitment in the one secular sphere, undercommitment in others;

voluntary renunciation of time-conditioned privileges in the educational system, etc.

2. Deliberately unpretentious and realistic undertakings, in order as Christians to contribute to the solution of important problems of the time wherever and insofar as the gospel of Jesus Christ itself is unambiguously involved (the racial question, overpopulation, reconciliation of nations, social distress, and so on). It would be a question, not so much of institutionalizing as far as possible every initiative and undertaking of the Church in the secular sphere, as of acting as a mobile "fire-service" wherever and as long as a special effort is required.

So much for the suggestions for reform under discussion. With a view to rapid realization of these, it is naturally all the pastors in the Church primarily, the bishops in particular, who are addressed. The Church today certainly no longer needs the formalistic authority of former times, based simply on a particular title or a special position: this kind of authority has reached a serious crisis; and rightly so. But the Church does indeed need pastors possessed of genuine, intrinsic authority, based on competence for the matter in hand, on human qualities and on the will to co-operate in partnership. For a planned realization of renewal in the Church we need a spiritual leadership. A vacuum of authority, such as can be seen frequently in the Church today and which cannot be filled by theology alone—although this has its own specific authority—must in the long run have very corrupting effects and create a favorable situation for fanatical extremism. Only open-minded, perspicacious, energetic pastors, who proceed resolutely in the vanguard, can help the Church of today; not distrustful and timid brakesmen, bringing up the rear.

People will ask how a theologian can be so bold as to put forward these numerous and far-reaching suggestions for reform. I have referred to my book *The Church,* in which the exegetical, historical, theological-systematic foundations for the reforms cited are thoroughly explained. But this is not the decisive factor. For pastors, teachers, and all members of the Church, the fundamental question arises: Why should the renewal take just this turning?

When is the Church really on the right road? And if in the past she was clearly not always on the right road, how can she be certain of being so in the future? When is the Church established for the future in that truth on which all truthfulness must be intent?

The above suggestions would not be rightly understood if it were thought that the Church would preserve the truth for the future by adapting herself to the present. Certainly she must do this. Certainly today it is a question of *aggiornamento*. But there is a false adaptation to the present, to the world: there can be an adaptation to evil, to anti-God forces, to what is alien to God in this world and at the present time. A Church thus adapting herself would capitulate to the prejudices of the present age, would become untruthful, would not have the future for herself. To her the words of the apostle Paul would apply: "Do not be conformed to this world but be transformed by the renewal of your mind, that you may prove what is the will of God, what is good and acceptable and perfect" (Rom 12:2).

But neither can the contrary be admitted: that the Church preserves the truth for the future by holding firmly to the past. Certainly she must do this too. Certainly it is a question today of a re-form, of taking up an earlier form. But there is a false attachment to the past, when people are attached precisely not to what is good and acceptable and perfect in the past; if they want to stick to the past only through laziness and sloth. This false attachment to the past is no less dangerous than false adaptation to the present. For in fact attachment even to something good can be false. This is the case when the human is placed above the divine, the commandment of man above the commandment of God, the tradition of man above the word of God. A Church so attached to the old would slip back into the narrow views of a bygone age; she would become untruthful and would not possess the future for herself. To her would apply the words of Jesus: " 'You leave the commandment of God, and hold fast to the tradition of men.' And he said to them, 'You have a fine way of rejecting the commandment of God, in order to keep your tradition, . . . thus making

void the word of God through your tradition which you hand on' "
(Mk. 7:8–9, 13).

We see then that the Church is not on the right road, not established in truth for the future, simply by being adapted to the present. This can lead to modernism. But neither will she be so established by sticking to the past. This can lead to traditionalism. And the question becomes so much more urgent: when, then, is she on the right road? What is the criterion, the rule, for this?

The Church is established in truth for the future by having behind her in each new age the gospel of Jesus Christ himself. The criterion, therefore, is the gospel of Jesus Christ, attested by the apostolic Church. For the Church did not emerge spontaneously. God himself called her out as the *ecclesia,* called from the world, from men. God himself has called her out, through this call which went out in Jesus, the Christ. This call is a *euangelion,* a joyful message; the message of God's sovereignty over this world; the message that man is to be so radically committed for God that he is at the same time committed for men; the message of God's love to men and man's love to God and men. This message, which Jesus himself exemplified up to his death and into his new life, is what challenges the faith and devotion of man. This message of Jesus Christ has constantly been received with faith, from this message of the living Lord the Church came to be: the Church as the community of those who believe and love, who put their whole trust in their Lord ascended to God and who are journeying through this present time to the absolute future of the kingdom of God.

The Church is established in the truth only as the pilgrim people of believers, not of seers. The Church, as consisting of human beings, must constantly be journeying through the desert, through the darkness of untruth and untruthfulness. In details she lapses constantly into this untruth and untruthfulness. And therefore she must constantly orient herself afresh, renew herself in truth and truthfulness. Constantly she must seek afresh the new way into an unknown future. But no matter how great the darkness may be, the Church has always a final guiding star, as the ancient people of God too had already a guiding star through the desert: God's word that constantly brings us afresh into the truth. In these last times God's definitive word has become manifest in Jesus, the Christ. This word of God in Jesus Christ, as the Apostolic Church shows in her original testimony, is the Church's guiding star, in the light of which she can orient herself in the errors and confusion of the times.

If the Church has behind her the message of Jesus Christ himself, then she is on the right road, she is established in the truth. If the Church has behind her the message of Jesus Christ himself, then in a new age she may—indeed, in a new age, she frequently must —come to a turning point, precisely in order to remain faithful to the original message in changing times. This message does not bind her to a past that is over and done with, but to the future freshly approaching each day. The Christian message must thus, with an eye on the future, be translated in word and deed into the present that is constantly new. And thus the Church must understand, precisely in the light of the message of Jesus Christ, how to read the signs of the times. In the light of the message of Jesus Christ she will better understand also the new age, and in the light of the new age again also the message of Jesus Christ. And by the criterion of the message of Jesus Christ, which teaches us the right way critically to listen and observe, the principle then holds: *Vox temporis, vox Dei,* the voice of the time is the voice of God. And the Church as the community of those who believe, hope and love, is then truthfully the vanguard of God in mankind intent upon the future.

What gives us *courage* today for pressing suggestions of reform, however debatable they may be in detail? What should give us courage also for further necessary deeds of reform, no matter how imperfect in detail they still may be? The message of Jesus Christ itself, which in every new age again freshly challenges— must challenge—the Church.

And what gives us the certainty today that the Church on her new road of greater truthfulness is on the right road, really established in the truth? The message of Jesus Christ, on the truth of which the Church in our time has clearly been thinking afresh.

And what gives us today the calm and joyous *hope,* in spite of all failure, that there will never again be a definitive return to the old untruthfulness; in spite of all opposition, that the new movement towards greater truthfulness in the Church will prevail? The message of Jesus Christ which shows us—makes us see in a new light—the best of the new world: the new truthfulness in the Church is a response to the deepest longings and strivings of the new age *and* a response to the message of Jesus Christ itself. What belongs both to the new age *and* to the gospel of Jesus Christ in the Church will inevitably prevail against all contradiction and resistance, reversals and relapses, impediments and handicaps. The new truthfulness is the future of the Church. It must be grasped, not in fear, but with great gratitude.

APPENDIX ON THE QUESTION
OF BIRTH CONTROL: A HELPING WORD

In a situation which, within the Catholic Church, has often been marked by desperation, resignation, or opposition, the author has been called upon for a statement by the Swiss television program "Wort zum Sonntag" ("The Word on Sunday"). We reproduce here this brief statement of position.

ONLY this afternoon I have been asked, by way of exception, to give this short talk this coming Sunday. The Encyclical of Pope Paul VI on Birth Control, along with the Czechoslovakian struggle for freedom, absorbed world opinion above all else, and it can therefore not be ignored on this Sunday program.

In five minutes one cannot say much about it. One can certainly not weigh arguments and counter arguments. Neither can one analyze the situation. Some points have already been clarified in the public discussions of the last few days.

1. This encyclical is the authentic expression of an *ex-officio* papal position taken at the end of prolonged reflection. It would be an illusion to suppose that it might be withdrawn or corrected in the foreseeable future.

2. This position is *fallible*. Rome admits this.

3. It has—amazing to Rome—come into collision with the unanimous rejection of world opinion outside the Catholic Church, and it has, at the same time, precipitated within the Catholic Church

183

the most acute internal crisis of the last decades. Many within the Church—including bishops, theologians, pastors, and lay men and women—are shaking their heads, are full of doubt, are desperate; many are contradicting its teaching in public. The Pope saw himself as under the necessity of defending his encyclical immediately after its publication; and in many countries the bishops' conferences are meeting to try to find a way out.

In this trying hour of the Catholic Church, in which we are moreover dependent on the understanding and help of Protestant Christians, we must try to say a helping word. What shall we do? How shall we go on?

First: It *will* go on—the Catholic Church with its renewal, with its growth in ecumenical understanding. You must make no mistake about that. You must not abandon hope. We shall overcome this crisis as we have overcome many before it—and this one, if I see it correctly, even with profit. The primary argument for the Pope was that he felt bound ex-officio to the definite teaching given by his predecessors and to that of the episcopacy of the early part of the century. That fact should guide our church to a critical examination of the concept of authority and of the teaching role, the formulation of dogma and especially the question of infallibility. Should it not be that in the future Church infallibility will be found less in statements and doctrines and much more in the conviction of the faith: that the Church is sustained by the Spirit of God and will always be renewed *in spite of* all errors and *through* all errors, whether of popes, bishops, theologians, pastors, lay men and women? It is questions like this that we must now raise, along with the Protestant Christians, who, on their side, are not free of the problem of contradictions in their teaching. They must pose the same questions—through, perhaps, from a different direction. This will be of great assistance to the rapprochement between us.

The Church will, therefore, go on. *And what do we have to do?* Three things.

1. We must take the papal decision of conscience seriously and accord it our respect.

2. We must ponder his arguments and discuss them in loyalty. This does not mean brushing aside our doubts; we must voice them, to help ourselves and the Church towards clarity. We will not judge one another but try to understand one another.

3. Those among us who, after deep and serious reflection upon themselves, their marriage partner and God, have come to the view that in order to preserve their love and the happiness of their marriage they must act otherwise than the encyclical states are not, according to the traditional teaching—which binds the popes as well—committing sin. They must follow their own consciences. When you act according to the best of your knowledge in the light of your conscience, you must not indict yourself for sin. You must quietly and, in accordance with your conviction, certainly participate in the life of the Church and its sacraments. You can surely count on the understanding of your confessor. It will therefore depend on each one of us whether the Church comes out of this crisis with a new maturity and sense of responsibility. And this will help not only our church but all churches.